KU-169-982

STUDENTS' GUIDE TO LEGAL WRITING, LAW EXAMS AND SELF ASSESSMENT

Third Edition

Enid Campbell
Richard Fox
Melissa de Zwart

THE FEDERATION PRESS
2010

Published in Sydney by:
  The Federation Press
  PO Box 45, Annandale, NSW, 2038
  71 John St, Leichhardt, NSW, 2040
  Ph (02) 9552 2200 Fax (02) 9552 1681
  E-mail: info@federationpress.com.au
  Website: http://www.federationpress.com.au

National Library of Australia
Cataloguing-in-Publication entry
        Students' guide to legal writing, law exams and self assessment / Enid
    Campbell, Richard Fox, Melissa de Zwart

    3rd ed.
    Includes index.
    ISBN 978 186287 755 9 (pbk)

    Legal composition – Textbooks.
    Law examinations – Textbooks.

808.06634

©   The Federation Press and contributors
    This publication is copyright. Other than for the purposes of and subject to the
    conditions prescribed under the Copyright Act, no part of it may in any form or
    by any means (electronic, mechanical, microcopying, photocopying, recording
    or otherwise) be reproduced, stored in a retrieval system or transmitted without
    prior written permission. Enquiries should be addressed to the publishers.

Typeset by The Federation Press, Leichhardt, NSW.
    Printed by Ligare Pty Ltd, Riverwood, NSW.

This book has been printed on paper certified by the
Programme for the Endorsement of Forest Certification
(PEFC). PEFC is committed to sustainable forest management
through third party forest certification of responsibly
managed forests.

Preface

This book offers general advice to undergraduate law students and students of legal studies regarding the preparation and presentation of assessable written work and law examinations. It offers a check list of the basic research skills students should possess at the end of their first year. The work is directed chiefly to students in their first year of tertiary study, but will also be helpful to those in later years. It offers practical guidance in an affordable and concise form.

This third edition contains additional advice on how to avoid the dangers of excessive and uncritical reliance on the rich world of the internet in writing assignments and includes helpful check lists for readers to determine whether their approach to legal research and study in this important first year is likely to produce success.

In presenting written work in law subjects, students are expected to express themselves in a lucid, logical, concise and persuasive fashion. They are also expected to follow basic conventions of legal writing. Not all of these conventions are peculiar to legal writing. A number of them are common to many scholarly disciplines. But the discipline of law has its own conventions and the learning of them is an essential part of learning to write in a lawyer-like manner, whether in a critical essay, a comment on some aspect of law, an answer to a legal problem, or recommendations for law reform.

Part 1 is about the process of writing, beginning with preliminary tasks such as deciding the purpose and scope of the writing task, preparation of a provisional plan for the finished work and the gathering and recording of material to be utilised in that work. Practical steps in a systematic and self-critical approach are described. If followed, these will do much to ease the task of preparing and presenting written assignments and improving the quality of final submissions.

Parts 2 and 3 are largely about the conventions of legal writing. In these Parts special attention is given to electronic sources in legal research and 'medium neutral' citation forms for judgments and other sources initially only available on the internet.

Part 4 seeks to build the confidence of students facing the different types of formal law exams for the first time. It deals with pre-exam preparation as well as the important issues of timing, relevance, and writing style in the exam itself. All students aspire to do well in their exams. This will assist in realising that goal.

The guide is not meant to be a manual on legal research, nor does it aim to compete with the more comprehensive texts on writing, style, forms of citation, and exam preparation and technique. A list of works of that kind is to be found in Part 5.

The new Part 6 on Self Assessment contains a check list of the research skills that should have been acquired in the first year and one which tests whether students have adopted successful study practices and have attitudes conducive to success in law.

We are grateful to Kay Tucker, Manager of the Monash University Law Library and Patricia Hughes, its Learning Skills Advisor who gave us the benefit of their sound advice and experience as did Janet Smith, Manager of Information Services of the Australian Institute of Criminology. Thanks also to Ann Cunningham at Federation Press and her contacts for helpful suggestions for improvements in this edition.

Enid Campbell AC, OBE
Emeritus Professor
Faculty of Law, Monash University

Richard G Fox AM
Emeritus Professor,
Faculty of Law Monash University

Melissa de Zwart
Associate Professor
School of Law, University of South Australia

Contents

CONTENTS

Academically-minded students plan their research and record their queries so they can run them across multiple sources. Others just rely on one or two 'tried and trues' and are likely, as a consequence to get caught out when these do not deliver, or contain errors ... the more 'Googlecentric' of them never plan research strategies. The structures of web-based search engines don't invite careful planning; they invite surfing and consequentially a reliance on serendipity.

Talbot-Stokes, R, '"Scuse me Miss! What's an Unreported Judgment?":
Relating Graduate Attributes to Legal Research Skills in the Workplace'
(2008) 16(4) *Australian Law Librarian* 264-269 at 264

PART 1

Preparing Written Work

The order in which the material in this part is presented is intended to serve as a check list of the steps which should be taken in the preparation of written work for assessment. The advice offered encourages the use of a systematic and self critical approach to the task of writing.

1.1 Decide the Purpose and Scope of the Writing Task

1.1.1 Type of Exercise

As a student of law or legal studies the written work you may be required to submit for formal assessment can take a variety of forms, for example:

- A discursive essay similar to an article published in a legal journal.

- A case comment, that is, a critical commentary on a particular judicial decision.

- An answer to a legal problem, perhaps in the form of an opinion of counsel or a judge.

- An exercise in law reform involving critical analysis of the current law and practice in relation to a particular subject, exploration of options for change, and recommendations.

This book does not deal in legal drafting exercises, nor letters of advice to clients. Writing answers to exams is dealt with in **Part 4**.

1.1.2 Purpose

Whatever form they take, written exercises have two objectives, one narrower, the other wider. The narrower one requires that you

LIVERPOOL JOHN MOORES UNIVERSITY
LEARNING SERVICES

address the specific questions posed in the problem, essay or assignment. You must clearly understand what these are before you begin. For instance, you may be asked to advise only one of a number of parties; or to act for the plaintiff rather than the defendant; or even to play the role of a judge. The question or problem may expressly or implicitly require you to undertake an analysis of the social policy behind the law, or to make comparisons between one jurisdiction and another. You must always squarely address questions and issues that have been directly posed.

The broader purpose that underlies each of the various forms of exercise is to provide you with an opportunity to demonstrate whether you possess skills in analysis, research, logic, persuasion and creative argument. It is not enough for you to produce the 'right' answer (for there may be none); in assessment, the quality of the underlying research and supporting argumentation carries far more weight.

1.1.3   Length

You should comply with the specific word limits set for the assignment, or risk being penalised in the grade allocated. Footnotes and bibliographies may count as words. Appendices consisting of extracts, newspaper cuttings, statistical tables and other material not forming a direct and integral part of the line of argument ordinarily do not count. Check with your lecturer whether such material will be accepted and how it is to be treated in the word count.

Where no specific word maximum has been set, you should confirm the applicable limit with your lecturer. If you insist on handing in written work which significantly exceeds the prescribed word limit, you must expect that a deduction from the normal grade that would have been allocated will be made in fairness to those students who have complied with the word limit. If you knowingly submit written work which falls well below the word limit, do not be surprised if you are failed, or otherwise downgraded, for having covered the topic inadequately.

1.1.4   Date Due

You will be expected to submit work by the due date. Timeliness is an essential part of legal practice. For a lawyer the sanctions for delay may include increased legal costs, the possibility that further proceedings will be barred, or disciplinary action by the relevant professional body. For a law student late submission of written work may result in a reduction of the grade that might otherwise have been earned because the extra time represents an unfair advantage over those who submit on time. It may lead to an absolute refusal to accept the out-of-time assignment and complete loss of the allocated marks. If persuasive reasons for the delay exist, and the lecturer expressly consents, a short extension of time for submission of written work may be possible.

> *Applications for extension of time should ordinarily be made in writing with supporting evidence. Seek the advice of your lecturer regarding the procedures for any such application.*

1.1.5   Allow Sufficient Time

Time must be allowed for planning, research, thinking, writing, revision, rewriting and the ordinary unexpected exigencies of life, for example, minor illness, etc. Allowance must also be made for time to complete assignments, essays and examinations scheduled in other subjects. It is wise to maintain an electronic calendar or written diary which not only shows your social and lecture commitments, but also the dates on which your written work is due and the days you have allocated for researching it, preparing a first draft, refining it and handing in the final version. Good students have learnt good time management; poorer students stumble from one last-minute time crisis to another. Do not assume that all outstanding written work can be completed over short periods, for example, weekends, or during the Easter break. Beware of procrastination. You must allow time for reflection on your work in progress. This permits you to develop a better perspective of its structure and content. Your first draft should always be put aside for some days, perhaps up to a week, before reviewing it prior to assembling the final version.

Recognising that you are procrastinating will help you cut short the dawdling that will end up in a frenzy of last minute activity.

Ask yourself:
*Am I viewing this assignment negatively as confusing, threatening and onerous rather than challenging, rewarding and the opportunity for a good grade? [**Action:** Ask the lecturer to clarify the confusing elements, then put on paper the main headings under which you think you may write.]*

*Am I being distracted by activities like games, social networking sites, and instant messaging that are accessible via my computer? [**Action:** The computer can be your enemy as well as your friend in giving you a start on the assignment. When it is distracting you from starting, switch it off! Write on a sheet of paper the main issues which you think you must address. These issues may be turned into headings. Once you have got that start you can return to the computer to open a file and enter the main headings you have identified. Now focus on looking for legal indexes and full text periodical articles available via the internet that can offer you an overview of the issues raised by the assignment.]*

*Am I 'thinking' about the problem, but never putting any of my thoughts on paper? [**Action:** Write them down! Then sort them into an order that matches the headings you have sketched out, or re-order the headings to match the thoughts!]*

*Have I repeatedly promised myself to do something about the task 'tomorrow'? [**Action:** By following the above steps you HAVE made a start. Now write in your calendar or diary the specific time tomorrow at which you will continue working on the task. Schedule the times and places at which you will deliver on this commitment for the next week or two in preparing the first draft.]*

JUST GET STARTED
STICK WITH IT AND YOUR WRITING WILL EVOLVE

If you are still stuck in a rut, you will find inspiration by following the advice of Rao V, Chanock K and Krishnan L, *A Visual Guide to*

Essay Writing (Association for Academic Language and Learning, Sydney, 2007) (available free on the internet as an e-book at: <http:// dspace.anu.edu.au/bitstream/1885/47101/1/essay%20writing.pdf>).

1.2 Prepare a Preliminary Plan

1.2.1 Reasons for a Preliminary Plan

Most of the written work you will be required to present will be work of a kind which obliges you to draw upon the knowledge which you have already gained through your study of the subject or unit in which the written work is to be presented. But often the task will have been designed so as to force you to broaden and deepen, not merely your knowledge, but also your understanding. You certainly should not assume that the task can be adequately performed merely by reliance on your lecture notes, sources to which you have been referred as essential or recommended reading, and the notes you may have made on those sources. Often the task will involve research on your part: searching for material to which you have not been referred by those who are teaching you.

Before entering on the research phase it is, however, advisable to prepare a preliminary plan, based on your present knowledge and understanding. This plan will represent a provisional outline of the finished work in which its constituent parts are set out in a coherent and logical way. At the same time it should assist you to identify the particular questions which you will not be able to answer until you do more research, reading and thinking.

1.2.2 Signpost with Headings

Lawyers use headings to identify the main points they are aiming to make. Your preliminary plan of attack should be organised under headings and subheadings. They are regarded as a desirable aid to a well ordered piece of writing provided they are an indicator of the structure of the underlying argument and not merely labels on apparently unrelated categories of information. Use of headings is a common feature of the reasons for judgment in the decisions of the courts. Even if you only have questions at this stage, use them as the basis of signposting your approach to the problem, for example, 'Does a private citizen have the power to prosecute?'; 'Is there a causation problem?'; 'What burden of proof rule applies?'; 'Does the Commonwealth have power to legislate in this field?' Often the terms of the exercise itself will provide an indication of the key issues to be addressed and thus suggest the main headings required.

Whether an essay involves problem solving or legal policy analysis, headings should indicate the key points in the argument and may be phrased as questions as above, or keyword statements such as, 'State versus Commonwealth involvement', 'Defences available to an internet service provider'.

1.2.3   Introduction and Conclusion

You must provide a brief opening statement describing the aim of the particular writing task, identifying the components of the problem being addressed, and the approach you will adopt to addressing the task. This should form part of your introduction. Failures to identify your approach to the problem and to clearly outline your argument are common weaknesses in student writing. You should also plan to draw the line of argument to a conclusion. The preliminary plan must always contain a place for these three elements even though, at this early stage, the full scope of the exercise is not plain and even tentative conclusions have not yet come to mind. You should demonstrate your understanding of and approach to the task by defining key words used in the question or instructions.

1.2.4   Does It Make Sense?

Take time to consider how each of the elements in your provisional outline relate to one another. You can expect that the headings will be altered and elaborated and their order modified in the light of what your research reveals, but it is wise to stop and think critically about what you have designed before entering into the research phase. Think about the logic of your proposed structure from the reader's perspective. After all, the task is also an exercise in communication.

1.3   Gather Research Material

1.3.1   Sources

The primary sources of the law are legislation (including subordinate legislation) and case law. These are accessible electronically via the internet, as well as in printed hard copy forms. Secondary sources include legal textbooks, encyclopaedias, digests, periodicals and indexes. Many of these are also available electronically. Information on how to use both hard copy and electronic reference sources and the strategy and technique of legal research is to be found in texts such as:

> Bott B, Cowley J and Falconer L, *Nemes and Coss' Effective Legal Research* (3rd ed, LexisNexis Butterworths, Sydney, 2007).

> Cook C et al, *Laying Down the Law* (7th ed, LexisNexis Butterworths, Sydney, 2009).

> Milne S and Tucker K, *A Practical Guide to Legal Research* (Lawbook, Sydney, 2008).

> Watt R, *Concise Legal Research* (6th ed, The Federation Press, Sydney, 2009).

1.3.2   Checklist of Sources to be Consulted

Assignments which clearly involve research will rarely indicate to students what sources they are expected to consult, or the research procedures they should follow. An assignment may not even specify the issues to be considered: for example in relation to the advice which should be given to a client who wants to know what legal remedy or remedies, if any, are available to him or her in respect of some action (or inaction) about which he or she complains. The terms of the assignment may nonetheless provide some clues about the kinds of issues to be considered. For instance, the terms of reference may suggest that issues to be considered are whether the conduct about which the client complains was unlawful under applicable anti-discrimination legislation, and/or under common law regarding liability to pay damages for tortious action.

Once the issues to be investigated have been identified, it may be advisable to prepare a checklist of the sources which should be consulted, and in what order. The first item in that checklist might well be up-to-date legal textbooks, legal encyclopaedias, or loose-leaf services. If it is apparent that the assignment will involve examination of legislation, the next item on the research agenda could be a search for relevant legislation and then for cases in which courts or tribunals have had occasion to interpret pertinent provisions in the legislation.

Thus if anti-discrimination legislation makes it unlawful for persons to be refused accommodation in hotels on the ground of their race, it may be necessary to search for cases in which the concept of race has been considered.

The initial checklist of sources to be consulted may need to be revised during the course of research. Discovery of relevant material through research of some sources may suggest that some other sources should be consulted. For example, if a search of textbooks and legal encyclopaedias reveals that the case of *Constantine v Imperial Hotels Ltd* [1944] KB 693 is clearly relevant to one of the matters to be considered – ie whether, at common law, innkeepers are obliged to provide available accommodation to anyone who seeks it – a fresh item to be added to the checklist will be a search of relevant case citators. Those citators should indicate whether the case of *Constantine* has been considered in later cases.

1.3.3 Hard copy or Electronic?

Libraries now provide both printed and electronic sources of information about the law. Familiarity with both sources is essential. It is necessary to consult electronic databases like library catalogues and various index services to identify relevant sources. These sources may be online, through online journals, but hard copy resources should not be ignored. Ordinarily, it is wise to start with a source that handles broad concepts or comprehensively covers the legal topic in which you are interested. In many cases that introductory material will be found in a textbook, or a government report, or major periodical article, rather than in specific legislation, or derived

8

from a series of cases. It is becoming more common to find that the full text of books as well as other documents that offer policy or conceptual overviews are available online as well as in hard copy.

There is no rule that one form is better than another, though it is recognised that electronic databases are more suited to a search for the specific rather than the general and the abstract. Efficient use of both sources of information in tandem will result in better understanding and thus better research.

Electronic searching has the edge when the question involves a unique term or phrase, a particularly uncommon case name, or other elements easily distinguished by a specific and unique designation. Electronic searching of terms that are in widespread use is counter-productive. Thus, an electronic search of the term 'trust', which is a word which occurs in many different legal contexts, will produce far too many responses to be useful. It would be better to select a book dealing with the creation and operation of trusts in different contexts, such as wills or tax planning, in order to target the area of interest. On the other hand, an electronic search for an unusual proper name, such as *Mabo*, is highly likely to produce case law, commentary and other references directly relevant to a leading Australian Aboriginal land rights case which is referred to by this name.

1.3.4 *Strength and Weaknesses of Electronic Resources*

The library's catalogue, or electronic indexes of journal articles such as *AGIS* (Attorney-General's Information Service), *APAIS* (Australian Public Affairs Information Service), *CINCH* (Computerised Information from National Criminological Holdings), *Index to Legal Periodicals and Books* and *LegalTrac* are search *resources* that will guide you towards *sources* (books, periodicals and other works) which provide an overview of a particular legal area. Initially it is best to restrict the search to sources published within the preceding five to 10 years. Legal encyclopaedias like *Halsbury's Laws of Australia* (Butterworths), or *The Laws of Australia* (Lawbook Co), can be consulted to gain an overview of an area of interest. Both are available electronically.

Naturally the temptation will be to rely on familiar tools such as the leading search engine *Google* or the major online encyclopaedia *Wikipedia*. Whilst these are useful in quite different ways, they should not and cannot be your sole nor even your major source of legal information. You should recognise their serious limitations as methods of *legal* research. For example a general search on the search engine *Google* will generate a list of possible sources that does not discriminate between jurisdictions. Searching a particular term, such as 'copyright defences', will lead you to sources from the USA, UK, New Zealand and anywhere else that has copyright law, as well as Australia. You would therefore need to be very careful in relying upon the overseas sources as authorities on the position under Australian law. A far more carefully drafted and narrower search inquiry would have to be utilised. Even then the product of a *Google* search will not discriminate between authoritative sources and commercial, biased or simply misleading ones.

Wikipedia, as a general encyclopaedia regularly updated by contributions from internet users, may be useful for providing background information or defining certain technical or obscure references, but, the expertise and accuracy of those contributions are not guaranteed. Note *Wikipedia's* own disclaimer:

Citation of Wikipedia in research papers may not be considered acceptable, because Wikipedia is not considered a creditable source.

See Wikipedia, Wikipedia: Academic Use <http://en.wikipedia. org/wiki/Wikipedia:Academic_use>
at 27 February 2009

Wikipedia encourages users to follow two simple rules:
- 'Do your research properly. Remember that any encyclopaedia is a starting point for research, not an ending point.'
- 'Use your judgment. Remember that all sources have to be evaluated.' (Source: Wikipedia: Academic Use, at 27 February 2009.)

These rules may be applied to all online research. Most libraries will provide access to online dictionaries such as *The Macquarie*

Dictionary or the *Oxford English Dictionary*, which may provide a more authoritative and relevant source for defining key terms.

When using search results generated by a search engine such as *Google*, you should be aware of the different search techniques or algorithms used by such search engines to generate search results. Many will place commercially sponsored links at the top of the list. You should develop your skills in entering search terms and using Boolean keyword searches (and/ or/ within 8 words etc). You should also carefully scan all the search results initially presented and not merely rely on the first one or two links on the list.

When accessing web pages identified by *Google* (including those of apparently reliable sources for legal research, such as government departments and NGOs) you should also be aware of the following:

- the tendency on web pages to oversimplify information to fit the format of the page, for example, a government body may oversimplify its responsibilities and powers, you should always look at the relevant enabling legislation for an accurate *legal* description of its tasks and functions;

- the currency of the information: government departmental responsibilities are rearranged and reorganised from time to time and web pages are not always maintained and rapidly updated to reflect this, whilst other web pages are preserved as historical references only, see for example the web page of the former National Office for the Information Economy <http://www.noie.gov.au>;

- the need to look beyond the home page to the wealth of very valuable sources which may be available as links on that web page to publications such as annual reports, discussion papers and latest information on statistics, programs and finances. Links are also often provided to other agencies with similar functions.

Again, be wary that the internet, unlike lawyers and governments, does not discriminate between jurisdictions. You can travel across virtual borders without being aware of it, and you should identify only those sources which are relevant to your task.

AustLII (Australasian Legal Information Institute) provides a valuable electronic resource that publishes the largest free-access internet collection of Australian primary and secondary legal materials, including legislation from all Australian jurisdictions and judgments from most Australian courts. All of the *AustLII* databases can be easily browsed or searched by keyword. The case law databases include the judgments of the High Court, Federal Court, Family Court, and the State Supreme Courts (amongst others), with many of the judgments, particularly those from the High Court, becoming available within a few hours of the decision being handed down.

AustLII is also one of the only places on the web to access decisions from tribunals and commissions, for example, the Victorian Civil and Administrative Tribunal and the Australian Human Rights Commission. Secondary sources include many well regarded Australian law journals, law reform reports, and treaties. See the list of available databases at: <http://www.austlii.edu.au/databases.html>.

However, it is important to note that the judgments on *AustLII* are in unreported form, ie they are in the form as sent by the court, so have not been checked subsequently for accuracy and do not contain the catchwords or headnotes added by the commercial legal publishers. Likewise, the legislation provided is not the official or authorised version, so it is wise to check the various government websites for these.

If searching foreign law, be aware that few other countries have a resource as sophisticated as *AustLII*.

1.3.5 Note Taking, Photocopying and Downloading

There is an art to note taking. The aim is not so much to produce a précis, as to record your *understanding* of the source material. Photocopying, printing or downloading entire cases, statutes or articles is certainly no substitute for reading them. It may be a convenient means of transferring the research material from one environment (library/internet) to another (home), but the material still has to be assimilated and interpreted. Photocopy or download material selectively.

Read and analyse your first set before lining up for another session with the copier or the internet. Your initial findings may put you on an entirely different track. Photocopying, downloading to your computer, or highlighting text with coloured pens is no substitute for notes based on understanding, summarising, extracting and reinterpreting key ideas and concepts in that material with a view to finding a use for them within the structure of your preliminary plan.

> *Writing on or marking the original printed library material which you may consult in the course of your research is unfair to fellow students. It devalues and eventually destroys original and valuable material. It usually distracts and often misleads later users. It is also the offence of criminal damage. In addition, within your university or college it is likely to be regarded as a serious disciplinary offence resulting in fines, suspension or exclusion from the institution in which you are studying.*

Unless handled carefully, downloading information for use in an assignment without keeping proper records of the source from which the information was obtained can lead to unintentional plagiarism. Plagiarism is regarded as a serious academic offence (see below **1.3.7**) and the concept is very broadly defined. For example, the current definition of plagiarism at Monash University is:

> **Plagiarism:** *To take and use another person's ideas and/or manner of expressing them and to pass them off as one's own by failing to give appropriate acknowledgement. This includes material from any source, staff, students or the internet – published and un-published works.*
>
> *<http//www.policy.monash.edu/policy-bank/academic/ education/conduct/plagiarism-policy.html> at 27 February 2009*

1.3.6   *Record Keeping*

The notes you take should include full details of the source from which the notes and downloaded material are derived and should be in such a form as to enable you to distinguish between those parts which are direct quotations from the source and those parts which are by way of paraphrase. Make sure your notes and file records are accurate from the start, otherwise your time will be wasted in having to repeat research and recheck sources. In downloading material ensure that files and documents are labelled in a systematic fashion. They should not only indicate the source from which the material was downloaded, but also note the date to which the research is current. This will allow you to return rapidly to the same database for any necessary updates before handing in your assignment. Databases that are online are likely to be more up to date than the printed sources of case law and legislation, however again, you should ensure that you are using the official and current version of the material, not all online sources are official sources. Care should be taken in navigating electronic databases, as they can represent both the historical view of legislation, as well as the most recent version. Recording full citation and bibliographic detail of statutes, cases, periodical articles and books is also essential to the requirement that, in written work, sources be always properly acknowledged.

1.3.7   Acknowledgment of Sources and Plagiarism

Knowledge is cumulative. You are entitled and expected to draw on the ideas of others, but the sources of the ideas must be documented. Providing references and citations to the evidence in support of your arguments serves two purposes. First, it allows the reader to locate the material to confirm the accuracy of your research and that the sources do support the point being made. Second, it is intended to make clear which ideas and words are your own and which have been borrowed from other people.

It is plagiarism to reproduce, verbatim, passages from cases, texts, articles or other writing (including that on the internet) without marking them by quotation marks and acknowledging their source by a citation. Plagiarism also includes paraphrasing another's work or ideas without acknowledging the source.

Submitting another student's research output or writing (or your own work which has already been submitted for assessment in another course) is as reprehensible as straight-out plagiarism. Such conduct, and plagiarism itself, is a form of cheating or fraud which is regarded as a serious disciplinary offence in all academic institutions. See Roberts TS (ed), *Student Plagiarism in an Online World: Problems and Solutions* (Hershey, PA: Information Science Reference 2008) (also available as an e-book).

Australian National Model Legal Profession Legislation competency standards for admission to practice (for example Victoria's *Legal Profession Act 2004*, s 1.2.6) which require an applicant to be a fit and proper person to be admitted to the legal profession, allow consideration of any academic disciplinary action that reflects adversely on the character of the applicant for admission. This includes plagiarism. Be aware that it is likely that your law school will keep records of and be required to report to your relevant admission body, any documents relevant to a finding of plagiarism. See also Bartlett F, 'Student Misconduct and Admission to Practice – New Judicial Approaches' (2008) 34 *Monash University Law Review* 309.

Legal Profession Act 2004 (Vic)
2.3.3 Suitability for admission
(1) The Board of Examiners must, in deciding whether or not to recommend that a person is a fit and proper person to be admitted to the legal profession under this Act, consider—
    (a) each of the suitability matters in relation to the person to the extent that a suitability matter is appropriate; and
    (ab) whether the person is or has been the subject of disciplinary action, however described, arising out of the person's conduct in—
        (i) attaining approved academic qualifications or corresponding academic qualifications; or
        (ii) completing approved practical legal training requirements or corresponding practical legal training requirements; and
    (b) any other matter it considers relevant. ...

> *(3) An education or training body must, at the written request of the Board of Examiners, produce for inspection or copying by the Board of Examiners any documents held by the body that are relevant to the Board of Examiners' consideration of a matter referred to in subsection (1)(ab).*

Students may work cooperatively in their research, but the material finally submitted for assessment must be each person's own writing based on their own significant research effort. In some circumstances a lecturer may be prepared to agree to receive joint submissions and to allocate joint grades for collaborative work. This must be expressly agreed to before the research and writing commences.

1.4   Prepare a First Draft

1.4.1   Getting Started

There are two problems which you may face in preparing the first draft of your written assignment. First, actually getting started, and second, finding the appropriate level at which to pitch your writing.

You might begin by preparing an outline for the first draft. If the assignment involves consideration of several issues or matters, your outline might list those issues or matters in what appears to be the most logical order, under appropriate findings and subheadings. The outline might include cross-references to relevant parts of the material you have collected in the course of your research and your research notes.

> *To overcome writer's block, recognise that writing is evolutionary. Your final polished version will evolve from your first imperfect attempts at setting out your thoughts and understanding. It is more important to get ideas on to paper under the general headings into which you have divided the task, than to hold up your thought processes while trying to refine the quality of your expression.*

It often helps to think that you are explaining the nature of the problem and its possible solutions to someone untutored in law.

The use of a word processing program makes the job of outlining your intended approach to the task and revising, expanding and reordering successive drafts much easier. It also provides templates for various levels of heading, assistance with checks on spelling and grammar, access to a thesaurus, and retention of proper sequencing of footnote references.

1.4.2 Communication

The aim of all writing is communication with the reader. Thus you should aim to express your ideas as clearly and economically as possible so that the reader can understand and evaluate them. The fact that the law about which you are writing is complex does not mean that you should write in a complex style. If you find that you are producing convoluted sentences, it may be that the thinking behind them is still woolly. Perhaps too many ideas are being run together in the one sentence. Try to separate them into a set of simpler propositions. The writing styles which you come across in the course of your studies may differ markedly from your own (often because they are a product of an earlier age). By all means adopt their better qualities, but do not slavishly emulate them. Develop your own style, with clarity as your goal. Your sentences should be brief, clear and unambiguous. If a proposition in a sentence needs qualification, use another sentence to explain it. Shorter sentences and shorter words should be preferred to longer ones. Avoid slang and abbreviations like 'she's', 'won't', 'don't' etc (unless they are part of a direct quote). Do not try to be excessively formal. Padding writing with pompous expressions, circumlocution, or language which is unnecessarily technical is unwise. Do not use terms like 'herein', 'hereinafter', or 'heretofore', or expressions like 'as aforesaid' in a misguided attempt to produce formal 'legal' writing.

Simplicity does not mean lack of variety. Draw on the richness of the English language. Use a dictionary to confirm the meaning of words. *The Macquarie Dictionary* and the *Australian Concise Oxford Dictionary* are preferred because they reflect common Australian usage. Use a thesaurus (a word finder in a dictionary form) such as the *Oxford Minireference Thesaurus* (2nd ed, 1999) containing

150,000 words, or the *Australian Oxford Paperback Thesaurus* (2001) providing access to over 300,000 words to suggest alternative words. Most word processing programs also offer a built-in thesaurus. In Microsoft *Word* use Shift F7 to open it.

1.4.3 Technical Terms

When technical legal terms are the most accurate way of describing a legal concept involved in your assignment, make sure you have selected the correct word or phrase and understand its proper use. Many similar terms have quite different meanings: for example, counsel/council; assure/ensure/insure; guarantor/guarantee/guaranty; in re/in rem; distrain/distress; per curiam/per incuriam, etc. There are many legal dictionaries which may be consulted for help. Two noteworthy Australian ones are *CCH Macquarie Dictionary of Law* (rev ed, CCH, North Ryde, 1996) and Butt P (ed), *Butterworths Concise Australian Legal Dictionary* (3rd ed LexisNexis Butterworths, Sydney, 2004) (this is the student edition which contains 10,000 definitions; the *Butterworths Australian Legal Dictionary* (1997) is the practitioner edition and contains 25,000 entries). The online version is available via the *LexisNexis AU* database as the *Australian Encyclopaedic Legal Dictionary.*

American legal dictionaries such as Garner B, *Dictionary of Modern Legal Usage* (2nd ed, Oxford University Press, New York, 1995) and Garner B, (editor in chief) *Black's Law Dictionary* (8th ed, Thomson/ West, St Paul, MN, 2004) can be useful in providing more detailed information on legal usage than is contained in a conventional legal dictionary.

Legal words and phrases which are in the definition sections of statutes and which have been interpreted by the courts are to be found in *Australian Legal Words and Phrases* (Butterworths) in print and electronic versions. The main legal encyclopaedias such as *Halsbury's Laws of Australia* (Butterworths), or The *Laws of Australia* (Lawbook Co) have a section on words and phrases that have been defined or discussed by the courts, but are not frequently updated. Digests also usually list such words and phrases. For instance, *The Australian Digest* (3rd ed) provides a separate volume dealing with Australian

Words and Phrases. Words and phrases which do not appear in these publications can still be tracked down through an electronic search of full-text legal databases. *AustLII* (Australian Legal Information Institute – <http://www.austlii.edu.au> see above **1.3.4**) is a good starting point for such searches, particularly for recent definitions.

1.4.4   Comply with a Style Guide

There are certain minimum standards that must be adhered to in the presentation of written work. Some relate to the physical layout of the presented work. Others pertain to the style of the text and the referencing system to be adopted when citing the sources relied upon in the written assignment. Books and periodicals show considerable variation between themselves in the style they adopt. Guides on citation and referencing also vary. For instance, some style guides ask for the full first name of an author to be supplied while others only call for first initials. Some that are content with initials want them to precede the surname, while others recommend that they follow. Of greater importance, however, is that each style guide makes an effort to remain internally consistent both in relation to the organisation and style of the text and in the form of the supporting citations. So should you. The objective of a style guide is not to make your life miserable, but to make your writing consistently clear and useful to those who are to read it.

The fact that this work has been prescribed or recommended by your lecturers means that the advice regarding style of presentation which follows in **Parts 2** and **3** should be adopted unless there is a good reason to depart from it. If you do choose to depart from it, or are instructed to do so, ensure that you are faithful to that variation throughout the entire written text.

> *It is also important that, from the very first draft, the citations found in your text and footnotes be as complete and accurate as possible in order to save unnecessary extra work when preparing the final draft.*

It will help if you store recurring citations in your word processor as a glossary (in Microsoft *Word* use *Insert/AutoText/New*). You will be able to use the *AutoText* facility to call up the details of cases, legislation, books and periodicals for insertion in footnotes whenever they are required without retyping them in full. Only page or section numbers may have to be changed. Once compiled, the footnotes will accompany any text that is relocated within the document in the course of revising and editing the assignment. Other word processing programs will have similar functions.

1.4.5   Draw Conclusions

It is important that, at the end of the first draft, you begin to produce tentative conclusions regarding the issues or problems posed. Your difficulties in formulating those tentative conclusions may highlight the need for deeper analysis and further research. Conclusions may come in various guises, for example: advice for one party or another; prediction of judicial behaviour; policy recommendations; forecasting of future difficulties, etc. If the conclusion requires you to predict how a jury or court might decide a matter, consideration should also be given to the effect of applying the relevant burden of proof rules to the facts of the case. Ultimately the assessment of your conclusions will be based less on your ability to discover the 'right answer' than upon a judgment of how effectively you have been able to advocate a 'solution' that advances the interests of the person or entity for whom you have been called to give advice. Remember that the resolution of one part of a problem may have implications for another. Spell out the alternatives and their consequences. When faced with conflicting authorities, or none at all, look for guidance in analogies with other areas of law and be willing to debate the merits of the competing policies which underpin the rival positions. Without a conclusion, your work remains incomplete.

1.5   Revise the Draft

1.5.1   The Art and Value of Self Criticism

There is a natural tendency in students, particularly those who leave matters to the last minute, to make their first draft their last. They are so relieved at having completed it, that they want nothing more than to submit it and get it out of sight. This is unwise. Revision is vital for effective writing. There is proven merit in putting the first draft to one side for a number of days so as to be able later to look at it anew and in a more detached manner. Before reading it, refresh your memory regarding the assigned task. Take a pen or pencil to your own work. Read it as though you were another person and ask yourself whether the manuscript you are now reading adequately responds to the problem posed. Is it lucid? Do its introductory passages provide a sufficient overview of the topic and how it will be addressed? Is the order of presentation logical? Does it show evidence of critical evaluation of the researched questions or material? Are the reasons for preferring one line of argument to another adequately articulated throughout? Does it draw conclusions? If what is sought is legal advice, has that advice been given?

> *It is natural to believe that, as you are the author, your work is without fault, but such optimism is rarely justified. Remember: revision improves quality and quality improves marks.*

Put aside the pain you have experienced in writing it, or the agonising prospect of having to reread and rewrite it. Reread the text actively and critically. Mark offending passages. On reviewing it, be prepared to move, discard or rewrite sections if they are poorly expressed, irrelevant, out of place, or otherwise fail to advance the objectives of the exercise.

Word processors lend themselves particularly well to this stage of revision for it is possible to mark the offending passages without deleting them lest you later change your mind. In Microsoft *Word* select *Tools/Track Changes*. The default setting for how the tracked changes will appear in the text is to be found in *Tools/Options/Track*

Changes. This will produce text that looks like – 'if the magistrate is satisfied of guilt ~~on the balance of probabilities~~ <u>beyond reasonable doubt</u>, the next question to be considered is whether or not to record a conviction.' Once you are satisfied with the alterations, the computer can be instructed to execute the changes and remove the marks.

1.5.2 Recheck the Internal Logic

As part of the revision, you must ensure that the conclusion pulls together the strands of your argument. Have the various elements been organised in a coherent fashion? Is the logic of your thinking apparent? If your assignment has been typed using Microsoft *Word's* in-built styles for different levels of heading, it is possible to collapse the entire text so as to reveal only the headings and subheadings under which the text has been organised (use *View/Outline* or *View/ Document Map*). This will allow you to visualise the structure of the argument, or the steps in the analysis. If lacking coherence or continuity these headings and subheadings can be amended and moved from one part of the document to another along with the accompanying text and its associated footnotes. Use of in-built heading styles also facilitates the automatic preparation of a table of contents (use *Insert/Reference/Index and Tables/Table of Contents*). Other word processing programs have similar functions.

1.5.3 Prune Length

You must try to keep close to the prescribed word limit. Too few words suggests that you have not sufficiently addressed the problem posed. Too many indicates that you have failed to write to the point and succinctly. If your text does exceed the specified word limit, you must reduce it either by way of précis or excision. Fairness to other students who have observed the prescribed word limits requires that those who exceed them be penalised in the grade allocated. Word processing programs will count the words for you.

> *Before revising your work back it up! Retain a complete copy of each earlier draft on a memory stick and keep it physically separate from the computer on which you are presently working, or use an online backup system. Also retain all hard copy versions of earlier drafts. Design a file numbering system which clearly indicates the sequence of revisions and identifies which is the most current version, for example, Draft01.doc, Draft02.doc etc.*

Also ensure that the version number and the file name appear on the document itself. It is also wise to insert the date of the particular draft. This can be done automatically in Microsoft *Word* by the commands *Insert/Field*, select *Date and Time* category and the field name *SaveDate*. By highlighting the Date field in the document and pressing F9 after the most recent save, the date will be automatically updated. Other word processing programs have similar functions.

1.5.4   Check Grammar, Spelling and Punctuation

If you are now satisfied with the substantive merits and length of the assignment, you should reread it for the express purpose of checking its grammar, spelling and punctuation. A useful test of prose style and clarity is to read the text aloud. Are the sentences too long or convoluted? Is the language inelegant or ambiguous? Most word processor programs have a function to check spelling; otherwise use one of the paperback spelling check books published by Oxford University Press or Harper-Collins, or a dictionary. Check that the use of quotation marks, commas, colons, semi-colons and apostrophes is appropriate. (Microsoft *Word* provides a *Spelling and Grammar* checker in the *Tools* dialogue box.) However care is needed when using Spellcheck as the word chosen by the computer may not be correct in context, for example the computer will not usually choose between 'form' and 'from', but accept either regardless of the meaning needed. Make sure that the spelling checker is set to English (Australia) not English (US). Go to *Tools/Language/Set Language/* to select the relevant language and switch on the spelling and grammar checker.

1.5.5   Check Consistency

Check for consistency in spelling, capitalisation, hyphenation of words, abbreviations and contractions, mode of citation and the method of ranking headings and subheadings in the text. See below **2.3**.

> *It is important to examine your footnotes for consistency of style and content. Do not just concentrate on the text when checking consistency.*

1.5.6   Bibliography

You should check with the lecturer whether a bibliography is required. Bibliographies should include books, articles and government reports consulted in the course of completing the assignment, as well as a list of cases and legislation. You should list primary and secondary sources separately. If a bibliography is not required, you should ensure that the full details of works cited and referred to appear in the footnotes. Use a clear and consistent format for all references.

1.5.7   Typed and Readable

Assignments are expected to be presented typed on A4 paper and be legible (ie not less than 10 point font size). There is no need to use colour in headings or for emphasis, but colour can effectively be used to clarify the meaning and interpretation of diagrams, charts or tables where these are pertinent to the assignment. Do not submit work that is barely legible because it has been printed on defective or almost exhausted ink cartridges. Make sure you have access to spare cartridges.

If you are having a major project such as a thesis typed profession-ally, the final draft sent to the typist for word processing should be accurate in every respect. The draft should contain as few as possible handwritten corrections and additions. If the manuscript is handwritten, it should be legible, and unusual names and technical words and phrases should be printed. The typist should have clear and full instructions about the style required, or an example to follow. The instructions should cover the paper size, the width of the margins, whether footnotes or endnotes are required, where page numbers are to be placed, what spacing is to be used and how headings and subheadings are to be presented.

1.5.8   Comply with Layout Requirements

The text should appear on one side of the page only, with a margin of at least 3 cm at the left. Footnotes should be placed at the bottom of each relevant page (rather than appear as endnotes) so that the reader can quickly identify the sources cited. Word processing programs have the capacity to place footnotes at the bottom of the page automatically. Ensure that there is consistency in the numbering system and format adopted for headings and subheadings. Use of in-built styles in word processing programs is strongly recommended.

Check that all headings are attached to the first lines of the paragraph which follows, rather than being left as 'widows' because of an inappropriate page break. In Microsoft *Word* this problem is automatically solved by highlighting the heading and applying the commands *Format/Paragraph/Line and Page Breaks* then check *Widow/Orphan control* and check *Keep with next*. All pages should be clearly numbered (use *Insert/Page Numbers*). Unless asked to do so, it is not necessary to insert the manuscript into a special folder before submitting, but make sure all pages are properly fastened or bound together.

1.5.9   Identification

Most faculties now require the attachment of a special cover sheet which calls each student submitting an assignment to certify by signature that he or she has not engaged in plagiarism in writing the submission and which supplies at least the following additional information:

- Name of the unit, subject, or course in which the assignment is set (and the stream, if any).

- The title of the assignment or other identifying description. If the assignment offered you a choice of topics or problems, the front page must make perfectly clear which one you selected.
- Your name and student ID number (unless some form of anonymity, through use of an allocated number has been specified).
- Date of submission.
- Word count (use *Tools/Word Count*).

If submitting your work electronically is permitted, you should ensure that the cover sheet is actually incorporated as the first page of the electronic file containing your assignment.

1.6   Check the Final Version

You should read the final version carefully checking for errors, omissions and inconsistencies. Are all the footnotes in place and numbered correctly? Are all pages numbered and in their correct order? Are all cross-references completed? Watch for letters, words or lines that have been transposed, omitted or repeated, brackets that have been opened but not closed, or punctuation marks and footnote indicators that are missing. If the final version has been professionally typed, the finished typescript should be checked against the final manuscript. If possible the checking should be done by reading over the typescript with the aid of a second person. If this is not possible, then reading the final version aloud can help find small but important errors. Any page that contains a number of errors should be retyped or reprinted, though small corrections may be added by hand if clearly printed in black.

> *When replacing individual pages, make sure that the continuity of the text is maintained. Sometimes lines at the start or the end of the page are duplicated or lost in the course of repagination.*

1.7 Retention of Written Assignments

A copy of the final version should be retained as security against loss of the original manuscript. You should also retain your original notes and early drafts until the assignment has been examined. If the work was prepared on a computer, not only should back-up copies be regularly made and burnt to a CD or stored on a memory stick, but hard copy printouts should be kept as a precaution against the material on the disk being accidentally erased or damaged. Back-ups should be clearly labelled and stored in a location separate from the computer. When your work has been marked and returned to you, it must be retained until after the publication of final results. You may be requested to return all your written work to your lecturer so that all the work in the subject can be reassessed to determine your final grade.

1.8 Submission

When submitting your written assignment for assessment, follow your lecturer's instructions regarding where assignments are to be lodged. The onus is on you to see that the lecturer receives the work to be assessed. You should check whether assignments sent by email or fax will be accepted – many institutions will not allow them to be submitted in this form. If difficulty is experienced in submitting an assignment in person by the due date, send the assignment by mail postmarked on or before the due date. If electronic submission is permitted, ensure that your name (or other required identifier such as cover sheet and student ID number) is included in the assignment document, rather than as a separate attachment or in the email from which it will become detached.

A selection of books on legal writing is set out in **Part 5** of this guide.

PART 2
Matters of Style

2.1 Quotations

2.1.1 Use of Quotation Marks

Quotation marks should be used in the following cases:

- To enclose direct speech. For example:

    Smith J said: 'Delay defeats equity.'

- To enclose direct quotations. For example:

    The statute gives a right of appeal to 'a person aggrieved'.

- For the titles of articles, lectures and chapters in a book or thesis.

- To enclose words introduced by terms such as marked, endorsed, labelled, entitled. For example:

    The cheque was marked 'non negotiable'.

    The term 'a person aggrieved' has a defined meaning.

    The box was labelled 'handle with care'.

- To enclose colloquial expressions, slang, words used in a humorous sense and coined words. For example:

    As usual, Lord Denning 'did his own thing'.

Note that in all the examples given, single quotation marks have been used. This is now the preferred practice. Double quotation marks should be used only in relation to a quotation within a quotation. For example:

> Smith J expressed the view that 'where a statute gives a right of appeal to a person who "feels aggrieved" by a decision, the right thereby given is not the same as that given by a statute which gives a right of appeal to a "person aggrieved".'

> *Where the passage quoted exceeds 30 words, it should not be enclosed in quotation marks, but rather set separately from the text as a 'block' quotation.*

The quotation should in such instances be single spaced and separated from the text above and below by approximately two line spaces. It is common to indent it only on the left, but it is acceptable to indent on both sides. The quotation should be paragraphed precisely as in the original, although the first sentence is normally not indented. For example:

> As native title is not granted by the Crown, there is no comparable presumption affecting the conferring of any executive power on the Crown the exercise of which is apt to extinguish native title.
>
> However, the exercise of a power to extinguish native title must reveal a clear and plain intention to do so, whether the action be taken by the Legislature or by the Executive. This requirement, which follows from the seriousness of the consequences to indigenous inhabitants of extinguishing their traditional rights and interests in land, has been repeatedly emphasised by courts dealing with the extinguishing of the native title of Indian bands in North America.

2.1.2 Position of Quotation Marks

The general rules as to the position of quotation marks are:

- If a punctuation mark is part of the quotation, it should be enclosed by the quotation marks. For example:

  > 'An election was called at short notice, purely for electoral advantage.'

- If a sentence includes a quotation, the full stop should be placed outside the last quotation mark. For example:

  > The Leader of the Opposition said that 'the election was called at short notice, purely for electoral advantage'.

LIVERPOOL JOHN MOORES UNIVERSITY
LEARNING SERVICES

2.1.3   Interpolations, Errors and Omissions

Quotations should reproduce the original exactly, subject to the following rules about interpolations, errors and omissions.

Interpolations in a quotation by way of editorial addition, explanation or substitution should always be enclosed in square brackets. For example:

> 'Smith [the plaintiff] had no cause of action.'

If there is an error in the quotation, attention may be drawn to it by interpolating '[sic]' immediately after the error. For example:

> Smart J took into account the argument put by counsel
> as to the defendant's family background, but considered
> that 'this did not have any affect [sic] on the conclusion
> that the defendant was fully responsible for her actions'.

'Sic', which means 'so' or 'thus', should not be used when the quotation uses spelling which is obviously archaic, for example, employé for employee. Nor should it be used to cure sexist language (direct substitution *is* acceptable – though it is *much* preferable to leave the original language). For example:

> A strike leader is liable for a fine of $500 a day for his
> action.

This may be quoted as:

> A strike leader is liable for a fine of $500 a day for [such]
> action.

When words are omitted from the middle or end of a quoted sentence, or a whole sentence is omitted, the omission should be indicated by three spaced full stops. If there is a comma, semi-colon or colon immediately preceding the words omitted, the punctuation should be preserved and placed before the omission marks. For example:

> None of the authorities cited, ... bears directly on the
> issue before us ... We can only be guided by what seems
> to us to be required in the interests of equity and good
> conscience.

2.1.4   Capitalisation

The first letter of the first word of a quotation should not be capitalised if it is related grammatically to the preceding words, notwithstanding that, in the original, the first word of the quotation begins a sentence. Similarly, if the quotation does not fit grammatically into the sentence of the text, the first letter of the first word quoted should be capitalised even though it is not capitalised in the original. For example:

> The Act provided that 'no person shall bear arms in a public place'. [In the original, 'no' is the beginning of a sentence.]

> What was really meant was summed up by Hodges J: 'A statute may suspend the operation of prerogative powers but not abrogate them.' [In the original, 'A' is not capitalised.]

2.2   Numbers, Quantities, Dates and Currency

Ordinarily isolated numbers of less than two digits (that is, 1 to 9) are spelled out, but numerals should be used in the following cases:

- When there is frequent use of numbers, as in discussion of statistics.
- When reference is made to a group of numbers, some under, some over two digits.
- For percentages, decimals, dates, exact sums of money, whole numbers combined with fractions, numbers combined with abbreviations, for example, 3 cc, 2nd ed, 8 per cent. (The word 'percentage' should be spelled out in full, for example: 'Complaints of delay in responding to correspondence account for a large percentage of those made to the ombudsman's office.'.)
- For numbering pages.
- Isolated fractions and ordinals should be spelled out. For example:
  one-fifth
  fifth person

31

twentieth century

But 109½

- Unless am or pm is used, the time of day should be spelled out. For example:

   At five o'clock the jury retired. At 6.16 pm the jury returned.

- Dates should be written in the following form: 5 October 1996. In the text the names of months should be written out in full.

- Never begin a sentence with a numeral, but spell the number out. For example:

   Seventy-five people attended ...

   Forty votes were cast ...

For further information, see Chapters 10 and 11 of the Commonwealth of Australia, *Style Manual for Authors, Editors and Printers* (6th ed, Wiley, Milton, Qld, 2002) (hereafter referred to as the '*Style Manual*'). The full text is available online at <http://www.dcita.gov.au/infoaccess/style_manual.html>.

2.3   Enumeration

When enumerating items in the text, either numbers or letters may be used. If the items run on from one another, the numbers or letters should be enclosed in round brackets. For example:

   The Act dealt with four types of offences: (1) rape, (2) indecent assault, (3) incest, (4) prostitution.

If each item in the enumeration begins on a new line, use one of the following: 1., (1) or (a).

> *Written work may be divided into sections, sections into subsections, and subsections into further parts. When these sections and parts are titled, care should be taken to use a consistent method of grading the headings.*

With current word processing packages, different fonts may be selected at the outset by the adoption of appropriate 'templates', to create a clearly graded hierarchy of headings and subheadings which is then maintained consistently throughout. Subheadings may be set flush with the margin and indentation of the first sentence of paragraphs may be dispensed with. Note that paragraphs should *not* be numbered.

For example:

I. VICTORIA

The Victorian law on this subject closely follows the English law ...

A. BASIS OF LIABILITY

The basis of liability is breach of duty care owed by the defendant to the plaintiff resulting in actual loss to the plaintiff ...

1. Duty of care

In determining whether the defendant owed a duty of care ...

(a) The manufacturer's duty of care

The starting point for any discussion of the duty owed by manufacturers to ...

(i) Intermediate inspection. When the manufacturer's product is one ...

2.4 Italics

Italics should be used for the following:

- Foreign words and phrases other than those which have become part of the English language or are common legal words or phrases, like mandamus and habeas corpus.
- Titles of books, journals where the title is given in full, pamphlets, newspapers. But in the case of newspapers, the definite article is usually not italicised, for example, the *Australian*, the *Financial Review*.
- Case names, including the '*v*'.

- Short titles of statutes (unless used in a descriptive way, as in 'the Evidence Acts in the Australian States', or, in the case of *subsequent* references, where very many references are made to the same piece of legislation within the space of a few pages).

- The names of specific ships, aircraft and other vehicles, for example, the *Titanic*, the *Southern Cross*.

- Words and phrases you wish to emphasise. When words or phrases in a quotation are emphasised in this way, there should be a note enclosed in round brackets at the end of the quotation to the following effect: 'Emphasis added', or 'Author's italics' or 'Italics mine'.

> *Underlining may take the place of italics, but do not use both underlining and italics.*

2.5　Abbreviations and Contractions

The word 'abbreviation' refers to a shortened form of a word consisting of the initial letter, or the initial letter followed by other letters of the word except the last one. Traditionally, abbreviated words have been followed by a full stop, for example, M.P. for Member of Parliament, ed. for edition, v. for versus.

A contraction of a word differs only in that the shortened form ends with the same letter as the word, for example, edn for edition, vols for volumes. A contraction of a word is written without a full stop.

Today the omission of full stops after abbreviated words has become increasingly common in many publications and is an accepted style of writing for a legal work. Thus, 'MP', 'ed' and 'v' and other abbreviated words may now be written without full stops. Furthermore, 'i.e.', 'e.g.' and 'etc.' may now appear as 'ie', 'eg' and 'etc'. It is important, however, that consistency be maintained.

Abbreviations and contractions should be used sparingly in the text. (The use of abbreviations and contractions in footnotes is dealt with in **Part 3** below.) The names of states, countries, organisations and months should be spelled out; words such as 'chapter', 'page', 'volume', 'line', 'column' also. If the name of an organisation is a particularly long one, or it is customary to speak of it by its initials, the usual abbreviated form may be used, provided that the full title of the organisation is given when it is first referred to and the meaning of the abbreviation is made clear. For example:

> A summons was issued by the Australian Crime Commission (ACC) pursuant to ...

When abbreviations or contractions have been used in the titles of cases, the abbreviations or contractions used should be reproduced exactly as they appear in the report of the cases, for example *ANZ Banking Group Ltd v Ramlock Pty Ltd.*

With some exceptions, titles should be spelled out (for example, Professor, Police Commissioner). Judicial titles may, of course, be abbreviated (that is, CJ, P, J, LJ, MR etc). It is also acceptable to use the abbreviation or contraction for Mr, Messrs, Mrs (and their foreign equivalents), Dr, St and Rev and Sr and Jr following names.

2.6 Capitalisation

> *Excessive capitalisation should be avoided, and consistency in capitalisation should be maintained throughout.*

Proper names and their derivatives and the names of particular institutions, for example, the High Court of Australia, are always capitalised. The names of classes of institutions or persons should not be capitalised except when necessary for clarity. For example:

> At that time none of the Australian colonies had a representative assembly.

> The State Act was found to be inconsistent with the federal Act.

> The Houses of the New South Wales Parliament have no power to punish for contempt of parliament. The Houses of the other Australian parliaments do.

The definite and indefinite article should not be capitalised unless they are part of an official name or part of the title of a book, person or institution, for example, *The Macquarie Dictionary*, The Right Honourable.

The first letter of the first word of an independent clause or sentence should always be capitalised. For example:

> The case raised two issues:
> (1) Did the defendant have authority to make an arrest?
> (2) Did he exceed that authority?

> What the judge ought to have decided was: Does non-user extinguish prerogative power?

It is customary to capitalise such legal phrases as the Rule in Shelley's Case and the Rule against Perpetuities.

(For further guidance on the use of capitals, see Chapter 4 of the *Style Manual* referred to at **2.2** above.)

2.7 Spelling and Punctuation

Spelling should be consistent throughout the written work. The forms of spelling should accord with those in the latest edition of the *Australian Concise Oxford Dictionary* or *The Macquarie Dictionary*. But passages quoted from other works should retain the spelling of the original, even if it is archaic. When referring to American institutions or organisations, the proper American spelling should be used, for example, Center for Behavioral Research, Department of Labor, Defense Department.

Where a spell check is run on word processed copy, care will need to be taken to reinstate original spellings in quotations.

Make sure that the electronic spell checker being applied by the word processor is checking against Australian or British spellings, not American ones.

The possessive and plural of proper names should be formed according to the following rules:

- The possessive of one-syllable proper names ending in 's' or another sibilant should be formed by adding an apostrophe and 's', for example, Jones's book, Marx's interpretation.

- Subject to the next following rule, the possessive of proper names of more than one syllable ending in a sibilant should be formed by adding an apostrophe, for example, Aristophanes' plays.

- The possessive of proper names of more than one syllable ending in a sibilant and 'e' should be formed by adding an apostrophe and 's', for example, Jarndice's suit, Alice's action.

- The plural of proper names ending in a sibilant, except those ending in a sibilant and a final 'e', should be formed by adding 'es', for example, the Crosses, the Perkinses.

- The plural of proper names ending in a sibilant and a final 'e' should be formed by adding 's', for example, the Joyces.

- The possessive plural of proper names should be formed by adding an apostrophe to the plural of the name, for example, the Crosses' books, the Perkinses' estates.

(On punctuation, see Chapter 6 of the *Style Manual* referred to at 2.2 above.)

2.8 Use of Brackets

2.8.1 Round Brackets

Round brackets or parentheses ( ) are used in the text to enclose parenthetical remarks, page numbers, and certain numbers or letters of enumeration. Long parenthetical remarks in the text should be avoided.

Round brackets are used in footnotes to enclose the date of a judicial decision or a journal when the date is not necessary to identify the volume of law reports in which the decision is to be found or in which an article is published. For example:

(1986) 160 CLR 572
(1995) 127 ALR 10

(1994) 99 Cr App R 26
(1966) 5 Syd LR 221
(2001) 75 ALJ 8
(2002) 26 *Criminal Law Journal* 38

Round brackets are also used in the footnotes to enclose information about the edition, publisher, place of publication and date of a book, the date of a statute cited by its number, and parenthetical remarks. For example:

(3rd ed, Lawbook Co, Sydney, 2002)
9 Geo IV, c 83 (1828)
per Hodson LJ (dissenting)

2.8.2   Square Brackets

Square brackets [ ] are used to enclose the date of a law report or journal which cannot be identified save by reference to the date. For example:

[1990] 1 Qd R 111
[1992] 1 All ER 255
[1993] QB 419
[1994] *Public Law* 269
[2002] *Criminal Law Review* 33

Square brackets are also used to enclose some insertion or interpolation in a quotation (see *2.1.3 Interpolations, Errors and Omissions* above), and to indicate that information supplied is merely a guess.

2.9   English Usage

Essays and assignments should be written clearly, concisely and with precision. Words should be chosen carefully and the use of clichés scrupulously avoided. Guard against excessive use of phrases such as the following:

Arguably
As far as ... is concerned
As regards
As to

At this point in time
Going forward
Hence
In regard to
In relation to
In respect of
In the case of
In the first instance
In this connection
In view of
It is submitted that
It cannot be doubted
It is abundantly clear
It may be stated with some confidence that
It may well be
It seems to be
It should be pointed out that
It will be noted that
It will be observed
It would follow
It would seem
Moreover
One might suppose
One might wish
Owing to
Relative to
There can be no question
Thus
Until such time
With reference to
With regard to

The method of presenting legal arguments in essays and assignments is different from that adopted for the presentation of legal arguments in a court of law. It is not appropriate, for example, to use such phrases as 'It is submitted that ...' or 'It is my submission that ...' or 'With respect, ...'. It is preferable to use the words 'I think that ...' or 'I believe that ...' or 'In my opinion ...' or 'In my view ...'. These words are also to be preferred to such phrases as 'I feel that ...' or 'My feeling is ...' or 'Black J felt that ...'.

On questions of English usage, reference may be made to any of the following:

> Burchfield R (ed), *The New Fowler's Modern English Usage* (3rd rev ed, Clarendon Press, Oxford, 1998).

> Gowers E, *The Complete Plain Words* (3rd ed rev by Greenbaum S and Whitcut J, Penguin, London, 1987).

> Meehan M and Tulloch G, *Grammar for Lawyers* (2nd ed, Butterworths, Sydney, 2007). See Chapter 3 on 'Effective Legal Writing'.

> Peters P, *The Cambridge Australian English Style Guide* (Cambridge University Press, Oakleigh, Victoria, 1996).

2.10 Use of Official Titles

When referring to a judge, use the judge's last name, followed by the initial or initials signifying the judicial title, for example, Gleeson CJ.; Winneke P. No comma should be inserted between the name and the initials. When referring to two or more judges, the relevant initial should be duplicated without a full stop between, for example, McHugh and Hayne JJ.

When referring to judicial opinions, the initial or initials signifying a judge's title should be used even if the judge has been knighted. One should write 'As Dixon CJ said' rather than 'As Sir Owen Dixon said'. However, in the United Kingdom the Lords of Appeal in Ordinary are referred to as Lord, and the Lord Chancellor by title and office, for example, Viscount Simon LC. The Lord Chief Justice of England and any judges of the Supreme Court of Judicature should be referred to in the same way, for example, Lord Goddard CJ (or Goddard LCJ), Lord Denning MR.

When quoting or describing what a judge decided or said in a particular case, always use the title the judge held when the case was decided, not the title subsequently held. When a judge has since been elevated to a higher judicial rank, the words 'as [he or she] then was' may be added in round brackets after the name, but this addition is not necessary.

When referring in the text to authors of books and articles, it is not necessary to mention their professional status, office or occupation unless such information is vital to the purpose for which the author or work is referred to. If, for example, reference is made in the text to views expressed by HLA Hart in *The Concept of Law*, one should ordinarily not refer to the author as Professor Hart or as Professor Hart, Professor of Jurisprudence at Oxford University. On the first occasion this author is mentioned in the text, the reference should be to 'HLA Hart' (the name as given on the title page of the book). Thereafter the author might be referred to simply as 'Hart'. However, if other authors with the name of 'Hart' are referred, 'Hart' should never stand alone but should be preceded by initials or the given name.

When referring to judges in their capacity as the authors of books or papers, use their ordinary names and not their official titles. Sir Owen Dixon, *Jesting Pilate* is correct; Dixon CJ, *Jesting Pilate* is wrong.

2.11 Cases

> *References to the law reports in which judicial decisions are reported should not be included in the text, but should be given in the footnotes.*

All that should appear in the text itself is the name of the case, with the names of the parties and the '*v*' italicised. If the name of the case is a long one and the case is referred to several times in the text, the name may be shortened in the second and subsequent references. For example, after having once referred to *Craig v South Australia*, the writer might refer to the case as *Craig's* case. When such a short name is used, the word 'case' should not be italicised, nor should the 'c' be capitalised. It is otherwise when the word 'case' is part of the given name of the case, as in *Shelley's Case* and *Slade's Case*.

If the written work is in the field of criminal law where many cases cited will be in the form of, for example, *R v Brown*, it is acceptable to use the shortened form of *Brown*. If the year in which a case was decided is very important, the year may be written in the text in round brackets after the name of the case.

2.12 Legislation

2.12.1 Statutes

Today the citation of legislation passed by Australian parliaments is by reference to its short title. Although the use of italics varies between jurisdictions, it is recommended that, for the sake of consistency, the method now used for Commonwealth Acts be adopted for all legislation, namely, to italicise the short title of the Act and its date, followed by the jurisdiction in round brackets, not in italics, for example, the *Crimes Act 1914* (Cth), the *Crimes Act 1958* (Vic). Note that no commas are used.

When an Act has been referred to in the text, for example, the *Evidence Act 1995* (Cth), and the Act is often referred to thereafter, subsequent close references may be cited without italics and without the date, that is, simply as 'the Evidence Act'.

Where similar legislation in force in the Commonwealth and/or in the various States and Territories is discussed, the first reference to the Acts should cite, in alphabetical order according to jurisdiction, the short titles of the Acts, their date of enactment and the relevant jurisdiction, for example, the *Evidence Act 1995* (Cth), the *Evidence Act 1995* (NSW), the *Evidence Act 1977* (Qld), the *Evidence Act 1929* (SA), the *Evidence Act 2001* (Tas), the *Evidence (Miscellaneous Provisions) Act 1958* and the *Evidence Act 2008* (Vic), the *Evidence Act 1906* (WA), the *Evidence Act 1971* (ACT) and the *Evidence Act 1939* (NT). Thereafter, where appropriate, the legislation may be referred to as 'the Evidence Acts'.

Legislation is identified in each jurisdiction by means of a number (for example, the *Evidence Act 1995* (No 2) (Cth), the *Evidence Act 1977* (No 47) (Qld), the *Evidence (Miscellaneous Provisions) Act*

1958 (No 6246) (Vic)), but the number of the Act should not be included in the citation.

The use of short titles for legislation is a relatively modern practice and in the United Kingdom older statutes were cited by their long title or by their number.

The long title is found at the beginning of the statute and sets out briefly the purpose of the legislation, for example, 'An Act to render valid Marriages solemnised in certain Churches and Chapels'. Many older statutes in England were given a short title by the *Short Titles Act 1896* and the *Statute Law Revision Act 1948*. See generally, 44 *Halsbury's Laws of England* (4th ed), para 838.

Before 1963, English statutes were numbered by the *regnal* year in which they were passed, and each statute was given a chapter number. For example, the *Australian Courts Act 1828* is numbered 9 Geo IV, c 83, which means the eighty-third chapter passed in the session of Parliament held in the ninth year of the reign of George IV. The *Australian Courts Act 1828* was given its short title by the *Short Titles Act 1896*. Earlier it would have been referred to by its long title, that is, 'An Act to provide for the Administration of Justice in New South Wales and Van Diemen's Land and for the more effectual Government thereof, and for other purposes relating thereto', or more conveniently by its number and date, that is, 9 Geo IV, c 83 (1828).

When a statute is numbered serially within a *regnal* year (for example, 2 Anne, c 7), the calendar equivalent of the *regnal* year may be found in *Guide to Law Reports & Statutes* (4th ed, Sweet and Maxwell, London, 1962), pp 21-33.

Since 1963, United Kingdom statutes have been numbered according to the *calendar* year in which they are passed (for example, the *Employment Act 1990*), and as in Australia it is not necessary to include the chapter number (that is, c 38) in the citation. It should be noted, however, that prior to the enactment of the *Calendar (New Style) Act 1751* (24 Geo II, c 23), the legal year commenced on 25 March rather than on 1 January. Thus, under the old style calendar, the date of the *Bill of Rights* (1 William and Mary, sess 2, c 2) was 1688, but under the new style its date is 1689.

Some statutes may have acquired 'popular names'. Where these are sufficiently well recognised they may be used as permissible alternatives to the short title, for example, the *Statute of Frauds 1677* and *Lord Brougham's Act 1850*.

References in the text to the sections of a statute and parts thereof should be written as follows: 's' (plural 'ss'), 'para'. Where these words occur at the beginning of a sentence, they should be written as follows: 'Section 2 provides ...'; 'Paragraph (a) of s 2(2) provides ...'. A reference in the text to a subsection should be written: s 26(2), not sub-s 26(2).

References in the text to parts and divisions of a statute may be abbreviated to Pt (Pts) and Div (Divs). As with sections and paragraphs, however, where these words occur at the beginning of a sentence, they should be written in full, for example, 'Part 10 of the Act deals with ...'; Division 2 of Pt 10 of the Act relates to ...'.

The parts of a schedule to an Act are known as clauses and are abbreviated cl (plural cll). Where a clause commences a sentence it should be written in full, for example, 'Clause 7 of Schedule 2 specifies ...'.

Where the provisions of a statute are quoted, they should be reproduced exactly as they appear in the statute book, and the numbers of sections etc should not be preceded by any abbreviations. For example:

21M. Confidentiality

A person who is or has been–

   (a) a mediator; or

   (b) a member or employee of a dispute settlement centre; or

   (c) a person working with or for a dispute settlement centre (whether or not for fee or reward)–

shall not communicate to any other person or publish any information or document acquired by the person by reason of being such a mediator, member, employee or person unless the communication or publication–

>   (d) is made with the consent of the person from whom
>   the information or document was obtained; or ...

The general instructions regarding quotations apply to quotations from statutes.

2.12.2   Delegated or Subordinate Legislation

The titles of regulations and other forms of delegated legislation are not italicised. Each unit is abbreviated as 'reg' or 'r' ('regs' or 'rr' in the plural), however, they should be written in full at the beginning of a sentence. For example:

>   The Copyright Regulations (Cth), regs 8, 9 ...
>
>   Regulations 8 and 9 of the Copyright Regulations (Cth)
>
>   ...

The titles of local government by-laws (nowadays called local laws) are also not italicised. Each unit is known as a clause and is abbreviated as 'cl' or, plural, 'cll'.

2.12.3   Bills

Bills before Parliament, too, are not italicised. Each unit is referred to as 'a clause', abbreviated to 'cl' ('cll' in the plural), which should be written in full at the beginning of a sentence. For example:

>   The Evidence Bill 1994 (Cth), cl 42 ...
>
>   Clause 42 of the Evidence Bill 1994 (Cth) ...

2.13 Avoiding Sexist Language

> *Sexist (or gender-specific) language should be avoided as far as possible.*

Various methods can be adopted to achieve this end. For example, the following sentence may be rewritten in several ways to avoid the use of masculine-gender words:

'If the candidate begins the writing of his thesis with a more or less clear idea of where he is going, he may find it easier to write his introductory chapter after completing the other chapters.'

By using double pronouns:

'If the candidate begins the writing of the thesis with a more or less clear idea of where he or she is going, it may be easier to write his or her introductory chapter after completing the other chapters.'

By using the plural instead of the singular:

'If candidates begin the writing of their theses with a more or less clear idea of where they are going, they may find it easier to write their introductory chapter after completing the other chapters.'

By substituting 'a/an' or 'the' for the pronouns:

'If a candidate begins the writing of the thesis with a more or less clear idea of where the candidate is going, it may be easier to write the introductory chapter after completing the other chapters.'

By using the passive voice:

'Where writing of the thesis is begun with a more or less clear idea of its direction, the candidate may find it easier to write the introductory chapter after completing the other chapters.'

It is now becoming acceptable to use the words 'they' and 'their' to refer to a singular noun in some circumstances. For example:

No candidate shall be entitled to an extension of time unless they ...

Each candidate shall submit their thesis ...

For arguments in favour of adopting this method of overcoming the traditional legal use of 'he' and the cumbersome use of 'he or she' and 'his or her', see Corporations Law Simplification Program, *Drafting Issues: A Singular Use of THEY* (Simplification Task Force, Attorney-General's Department, Canberra, September 1995).

Sexist language may also be avoided by substituting a capital letter for nouns and pronouns. For example:

'If C, having trouble with one chapter of the thesis, seeks advice from S, S may suggest to C several ways of overcoming the problem.'

Alternative words or phrases may also be used. For example:

juryman	member of the jury
policeman	police officer
layman	layperson
workman	worker
chairman	chair/chairperson

If gender-specific language cannot be completely eliminated without sacrificing good style or sense, masculine and feminine terms should be used impartially. Because the law reports often only refer to presiding judges by their surnames, be careful about the use of 'his honour' or 'her honour' unless you are confident of their gender. In the introductory pages of the bound volumes of the law reports the full names are given from which you may deduce the appropriate way to refer to them. Otherwise it is best to use more neutral language such as, 'The leading judgment was given by Justice Brown who ruled that ... '.

(For more information on non-discriminatory language, see Chapter 8 of the *Style Manual* referred to at **2.2** above.)

2.14 Avoiding Jargon, Weasel Words and Padding

It would not be appropriate in writing an assignment on police powers to refer to those who are exercising them as 'cops'. Nor are the people the police deal with 'crooks'. They may be suspects, offenders (or better still 'alleged offenders'), or more specifically alleged thief or rapist etc. Even when writing about a technical area of regulation such as in relation to information technology, at least explain early on in your paper the meaning of technical jargon that is used in a specialist field, for example 'broadband', 'fibre to the node' or 'digital divide'.

There are also a set of weasel words that are a form of managerial jargon which are characterised by deliberately understating or disguising the truth of what is being referred to. What was the author of the example below really saying?

'Realistically speaking, the bottom line is basically that we will evaluate the issue in its context, and basically commit ourselves to endeavouring to achieve a more appropriate scenario with better outcomes for all stakeholders'.

Quoted by Watson D, *Dictionary of Weasel Words: Contemporary Clichés, Cant and Management Jargon (Random House Australia, 2004), p 5.*

Watson complains that such words 'hide truth and slew or complicate meaning'. For example a person's death in a hospital becomes 'a negative patient outcome'. In a legal situation, if a person has been dismissed, do not use the weasel phrase that they were 'let go'. Likewise, why use 'going forward' when you really mean 'in the future'. If a tenant is to be 'evicted' it is not appropriate to describe the legal action as 'implementation of a re-location strategy'. Ultimately the danger in jargon and weasel words is that they represent obstacles to clear thinking and clear communication in expressing the product of that thinking.

For the same reasons, avoid padding your answers with vague and meaningless opening statements such as: 'The internet is very big' or 'The law creates many problems' or 'The search for justice has been a consistent feature of evolving human civilisation'.

PART 3

Notes and References

3.1 Purpose

> *Place your citations in footnotes, rather than endnotes. Footnotes are your insurance against allegations of plagiarism! They are used primarily to refer to the primary and secondary sources you have relied upon in researching the topic and which you are directly quoting, or generally relying upon, in support of the descriptions you are presenting or principles you are advancing in your research paper.*

Material which is subsidiary to the text may be set out *either* as numbered items at the foot of the relevant page, that is, as footnotes, *or* as numbered items at the end of the written work, that is, as endnotes. Readability is greatly facilitated, however, where footnotes rather than endnotes are used.

Footnotes and endnotes are used for citation of authorities and evidence, for purposes of cross-reference to other pages in the work, and for asides and comments not essential to the thought of the text.

Footnotes and endnotes should use language and data economically. They should not be lengthy. They should not be used for a 'mainstream' extended commentary, nor should they take the form of selected bibliographies of references which are of marginal significance, or which smack of 'showmanship'. However they *are* an appropriate vehicle for inclusion of a necessary but subsidiary line of argument or commentary, or to lead the reader to the main body of authority – cases, periodical literature, texts etc. But their *chief* function should be to indicate authorities or sources relied upon (for example, cases and legislation) or to show special indebtedness.

The following should be carefully documented by citations in footnotes:

- Facts or statements not commonly known or accepted.
- All quotations the source of which is not immediately apparent.
- Documentation of paraphrases which amount to quotation.
- Cases and legislation referred to in the text.
- Cases and legislation supporting statements in the text.

Well established principles (for example, that an agreement is not legally binding and enforceable as a contract unless supported by consideration) need not be footnoted.

When material in the text is drawn from a particular book or article, a general statement of indebtedness or authority may be made at the beginning with a footnote reading as follows: 'For the following material I am indebted to …' or 'The contents of this section (or paragraph) are based on …'.

3.2 Books

When a book is referred to for the first time the citation should contain the following items:

- The last name of the author (or authors) followed by initials.
- The full title of the book, in italics (or underlined).
- The edition, if revised (2nd or subsequent).
- The name of the publisher.
- The place of publication.
- The page, paragraph or chapter reference.

For example:

> Graycar R and Morgan J, *The Hidden Gender of Law* (2nd ed, The Federation Press, Sydney, 2002), pp 67-68.
>
> Fox RG, *Victorian Criminal Procedure* (12th ed, Monash Law Book Cooperative Ltd, 2005), para 1.1.3 (alternatively [1.1.3]).

> Chisholm R and Nettheim G, *Understanding Law: An Introduction to Australia's Legal System* (6th ed, Butterworths, Sydney, 2002), Ch 3.

If a book has more than three co-authors, the author entry in the footnote citation should be given the name of the author first listed on the title page followed by the words 'and others' or 'et al'. For example:

> Hill C et al, *Arrest of Ships* (Lloyd's of London Press, London, 1985).

If reference is made to a particular essay or chapter in a volume of essays, the citation should be in the following form:

> Williams CR, 'Placing the Burden of Proof', in Campbell E and Waller L (eds), *Well and Truly Tried: Essays on Evidence in Honour of Sir Richard Eggleston* (Lawbook Co, Sydney, 1982), p 271.

Some books include the original author's name in the title. This should be italicised as part of the title, and the edition and the names of the editors should be shown. For example:

> *Cross on Evidence* (7th Aust ed by Heydon JD, LexisNexis Butterworths, Sydney, 2004), para 13001.

The title of the book should normally be cited in exactly the same form as it appears on the title page. If there is a sub-title this should be included, at least in the first footnote in which the book is cited. Since titles and sub-titles usually appear on the title page without punctuation marks to separate them, it is often necessary to add punctuation, generally in the form of a colon. If the title is extremely long, the title may be shortened for purposes of citation by omitting all but the key words. For example, the title of the book of essays given as an example above may be referred to as *Well and Truly Tried*.

If the book is in more than one volume, use Arabic numerals for the volume. The volume number should immediately precede the title of the book; it should not be prefixed by the word 'volume' or 'vol'. For example:

> Maitland F W and Pollock F, 2 *History of English Law* ...

The abbreviation 'vol' should be used only when its omission would result in ambiguity. Note that the years of publication of different volumes in the same series are not always the same and that there may be second or subsequent editions of some volumes.

When citing *Halsbury's Laws of England*, *Halsbury's Laws of Australia* and *The Laws of Australia*, the title should be written as follows:

> 2 *Halsbury's Laws of England* (4th ed, reissue), paras 502-504.
>
> 6 *Halsbury's Laws of Australia* [110.2845]-[110.2855].
>
> *The Laws of Australia* 14.3: 19-22.

Online version examples:

> LexisNexis, *Halsbury's Laws of Australia* (at 7 February 2009) 85 Conflict of Laws, 'I General' [85-145].
>
> Thomson Reuters, *The Laws of Australia* (at 10 December 2008) 2 Administrative Law, '2.4 Judicial Review of Administrative Action: Reviewable Decisions, Conduct and Powers and General Grounds' [2.4.94]-[2.4.98].

(See also instructions under the headings **3.14 Later References** and **3.15 Cross-References** below.)

3.3 Classical Works

Classical works are usually published in so many editions that it may be desirable to identify passages cited not by page numbers in the edition consulted but by the numbered parts or sections of the work. When the work cited has been divided into books and the books into divisions, the books are indicated by small roman numerals followed by a colon, the subdivisions of the books by Arabic numerals. When a work is not divided into books, the divisions and subdivisions thereof are indicated by Arabic numerals. The division and subdivision numbers are separated by full stops and the subdivision number is followed by a comma. No punctuation is used between the author's name and the title of the work or after the title. For example:

Justinian *Institutes* ii: 19.6, 7.

Aristotle *Ethics* v: 10.

Aristotle *Politics* ii: 6.7, 8.

3.4 Articles in Periodicals

The general form of citation is as follows:

- The last name of the author (or authors) followed by the first name or initials.
- The title of the article in single quotation marks.
- The year of publication in round brackets (or square brackets when there is no volume number).
- The volume number in Arabic numerals.
- If the volume is made up of a number of separately issued parts and the pagination of each issue recommences at p 1, the part number should also be included in round brackets following the volume number.
- The title of the periodical (in italics or underlined).
- The page on which the article begins (followed by the page or pages referred to in the article where appropriate).

For example:

> Lee HP, 'The High Court and Implied Fundamental Guarantees' [1993] *Public Law* 606.
>
> McGrath G and Kreleger N, 'The Killing of Mary: 'Have we Crossed the Rubicon?' (2001) 8 *Journal of Law and Medicine* 322 at 323-325.
>
> Nash Y, 'Compensation for Victims of Crime' (2000) 74(11) *Law Institute Journal* 56.

Where the article cited is written by several authors, the author entry should be in the form prescribed for author entries for books, at **3.2 Books** above.

When citing an anonymous note or comment appearing in a legal periodical, the words 'Note' or 'Comment' should appear in place of the author entry.

The title of a very well known periodical, eg the *Australian Law Journal* may be abbreviated, in which case the abbreviated title is not italicised, for example, ALJ. However, to avoid confusion as to what legal or other journal is being referred to the student is encouraged to spell out *all* titles in full.

Publishers of legal periodicals usually set out the prescribed form of citation on one of the opening pages of the periodical. If there is no form of citation prescribed, then the full title should be used. If trying to identify what an abbreviation represents, help can be found in the Monash University Library's *Abbreviations of Legal Publications*, which is available in print and on the internet at <http://www.lib. monash.edu.au/legal-abbreviations>.

Journal articles in electronic form should be cited as per the print format if the journal is available in both print and electronic form. If the journal is only available on the internet, the URL and date of retrieval should also be included.

3.5 Cases

3.5.1 Medium Neutral Citations

A distinction is drawn between 'medium neutral' forms of citing electronic unpublished judgments and conventional means of citing cases printed in law reports. Since 1998 the High Court of Australia has incorporated paragraph numbers in the body of judgments and has permitted the citation of electronically stored unpublished decisions in a 'medium neutral' way. This was needed because the page numbers in such cases varied according to the software used to view or print the document. Embedding visible paragraph numbers in the document instead of relying on page numbers enables consistent citation of specific locations within it. This approach is now utilised by all higher level courts in Australia. The components of a medium neutral citation of a case are (1) the names of the parties; (2) the year the judgment was handed down; (3) a unique court identifier eg HCA for High Court of Australia; VCA for Victorian Court of Appeal (for a complete list see Stuhmcke A, *Legal Referencing* (3rd ed, LexisNexis Butterworths, Sydney, 2005), Appendix 3; (4) the judgment number as issued by the court; and (5) where required, a number to pinpoint a particular paragraph within the document.

For instance *Ryan v The Queen* [2001] HCA 21 at [74] is a reference to the 21st decision of the High Court in 2001 and the paragraph number that will take the reader to the commencement of the judgment of Justice Kirby. Medium neutral citations can operate in conjunction with conventional citation methods. Thus it is permissible to continue to refer to paragraph numbers instead of page numbers even after the case is printed in a law report series. Thus a reference to para 74 in any of the following printed reports of *Ryan's* case (2001) 206 CLR 267, (2001) 179 ALR 193, (2001) 75 ALJR 815 or (2001) 118 A Crim R 53, will take the reader to the same location in the case irrespective of the differences in pagination in the reports. The convention is to cite the paragraph number of a judgment in square brackets as in *Ryan v The Queen* above.

3.5.2   Conventional Citations

When a case has been printed in a law report series the form of citation should be that indicated on the half-title page of the law report or at the head of the table of cases or as part of the running heading of the pages on which the case is reported. When the name of a case has already been given in the text, the footnote should refer only to the volume and the law report series in which the case is reported and the page on which the report of the case begins. For example, having referred to *Ryan v The Queen* in the text, the footnote citation would be (2001) 206 CLR 267.

The following publications should be consulted for more details on the correct forms of citation:

> Melbourne University Law Review Association, *Australian Guide to Legal Citation* (2nd ed, Melbourne University Law Review Association, Melbourne, 2002). Full text available at <http://mulr.law.unimelb.edu.au/files/aglcdl.pdf>.
>
> Stuhmcke A, *Legal Referencing* (3rd ed, LexisNexis Butterworths, Sydney, 2005).

American cases should be cited in the forms indicated in the *ALWD Citation Manual: A Professional System of Citation* (2nd ed, Aspen Law and Business, New York, Garthensburg, 2003), or *The Bluebook: A Uniform System of Citation* (18th ed, Harvard Law Review Association, Cambridge, Mass, 2005).

See also 5.4 below.

When the year of a volume containing reports of judicial decisions is an integral part of the title of the volume, the year should be written in square brackets, for example [1962] 1 KB. When the year is not an integral part of the title of the volume, but is added for further identification, the year is given in round brackets. The year in the latter case represents the year in which judgment was handed down. When the volumes in a series of law reports are numbered consecutively, as in the case of the *Commonwealth Law Reports*, the volume number *must* be given to identify the volume.

If a case has been reported in more than one series of law reports, cite the authorised or semi-official series in preference to others. For instance, although significant judgments of the High Court of Australia can be found in the *Australian Law Reports* (cited as ALR) or the *Australian Law Journal Reports* (cited as ALJR) shortly after they have been handed down, the authorised reports are the *Commonwealth Law Reports* (cited as CLR). There is a longer delay before these are printed because authorised reports are ones that have been checked and approved by the issuing court before being published.

> It is not necessary to cite more than one series of law reports when referring to a case. Cite the authorised report whenever it is available. The authorised reports, such as the Commonwealth Law Reports, contain an opening statement indicating that they are authorised by the relevant court. Be consistent in the citation used – do not mix different citations to the same case and do not cite a case merely through a secondary source. You should always go to the source material for your citation.

When it is relevant to indicate the court deciding a case and the informed reader cannot infer what court decided the case simply by looking at the title of the volume containing the decision, the court's name can be given in abbreviated form, in round brackets, at the end of the citation. For example:

> *Berry v The Queen* [1992] 3 WLR 153 (PC) [indicating the Judicial Committee of the Privy Council].
>
> *Barclays Bank v O'Brien* [1993] QB 109 (CA) [indicating the Court of Appeal].

In case citations, 'p' or 'page' should never be used with reference to the page on which the report begins. Pinpoint references should be in the following form:

> *Spratt v Hermes* (1965) 114 CLR 226 at 259-260.

If the location of a specific paragraph is to be identified, the citation can take either of the following forms:

> *Re Wakim; Ex parte McNally* (1999) 198 CLR 511 at 571 [101], or
>
> *Re Wakim; Ex parte McNally* (1999) 198 CLR 511 at para 101.

Note that no comma is written after the date of the case or after the number of the volume of the report, or preceding the page on which the case begins.

Page references in the form '58 et seq', meaning page 58 and pages following, are too vague and should be avoided. When reference is made to consecutive pages it is better to give inclusive page numbers. The use of 'ff' should be avoided for the same reason.

3.6 Legislation

Statutes cited in footnotes should be cited in the same way as they are cited in the text. (See *2.12.1 Statutes* in **Part 2** above.) When an Act is cited by its short title and this title is sufficient to identify it, do not cite its number as well. The title of the volume in which the statute referred to is printed should not be cited unless the student is relying upon a translation of an English statute originally published in Latin or French, in which case the title of the volume should be written in brackets, italicised (or underlined), and placed at the end of the citation.

There is no standard form of citation of subordinate legislation, ie rules, regulations and local government by-laws. The citation should always be sufficiently detailed to enable the reader to turn up the reference with as little trouble as possible. If the subordinate legislation cited is not published in a separate series (for example, in the Commonwealth, Tasmanian and Victorian *Statutory Rules* and the volumes of the *Queensland Subordinate Legislation*), and the title or number by which it is cited does not clearly indicate where the legislation is to be found, the source should be written in brackets at the end of the citation.

> *When comparable legislation for different jurisdictions is cited in a footnote, the name of the legislature, in abbreviated form, should follow each citation, and the citations should be arranged in alphabetical order according to the names of the jurisdiction, as in the text.*

If necessary, the footnote should also make it clear that, except where the contrary is indicated, the further citation of sections after the abbreviated names of particular jurisdictions refers to the statutes in the footnote. For example:

Sale of Goods Act 1896 (Tas); *Goods Act 1958* (Vic) (subsequently cited as Tas; Vic).

3.7 Newspapers or Weekly Journals

Non-legal periodicals appearing daily or less frequently should be cited by title and date of issue even if the periodical has a volume number. Page numbers should then be given. For example:

Australian, 4 November 2001, p 11.

The definite article is not normally italicised (or underlined) even if it is part of the title, for example, *New York Times*. There are a few exceptions, for example, *The Age, The Times* (London).

When citing an article in a newspaper or weekly journal, give its title in the same way as you would the title of an article in another periodical, together with the author's name, if given. For example:

> Dancer H, 'Internet Spy', *Bulletin,* 11 May 1999, pp 84-87.

When citing a newspaper report of a case, write the name of the case without italics (or underlining). For example:

> Mondolo v McMillan, *The Age,* 25 July 2001, p 3.

3.8 Media Releases

It is common for government ministers to issue media releases electronically on the internet to announce newsworthy events falling within their portfolio. For instance those of the Federal Attorney-General are available at: <http://www.attorneygeneral.gov.au/www/ministers/robertmc.nsf/Page/Media_Releases>. When citing these adopt the following form, showing the internet link and the date the information was accessed:

> Australia, Attorney-General (Robert McClelland), *Discussion paper explores possible improvements to native title system*, Media Release 23 December 2008 <http://www.attorneygeneral.gov.au/www/ministers/RobertMc.nsf/Page/MediaReleases_2008_FourthQuarter_23December2008> at 5 January 2009.

3.9 Official Publications

3.9.1 General Rules

These include official reports of parliamentary debates (Hansard), legislative journals, votes and proceedings, parliamentary papers, command papers, and reports of official boards, committees and commissions. The general principle to be followed in citing such material is that the document should be identified exactly and described in such a way that it can be easily located.

> It is common, but not inevitable that government reports will
> be published electronically, as well as in print. It is not essential
> to cite the printed version if an electronic version is available,
> particularly if it is possible to provide a medium neutral cita-
> tion to the relevant passage (see 3.5.1 above for explanation of
> medium neutral citations).

When an official publication is cited for the first time, the citation
should always begin by identifying first the country, state or other
government district, and then the legislative body, government
department, board, commission etc. There should follow such information about the volume in which the document is to be found as is
necessary to locate that document. For example:

> Commonwealth, *Parliamentary Debates*, House of
> Representatives, 1 December 2008, p 11873 (Kevin
> Rudd, Prime Minister).

> Australia, Australian Law Reform Commission, *For
> Your Information: Australian Privacy Law and Practice*,
> Report 108 (2008).

> Great Britain, Law Commission, *The Forfeiture Rule
> and the Law of Succession*, Report No 295 (2005).

> New Zealand, Law Commission, *Suppressing Names
> and Evidence*, Issues Paper No 13 (2008).

> Canada, Law Reform Commission, *Immunity from
> Prosecution*, Working Paper No 64 (1992).

> Victoria, Parliament, Drugs and Crime Prevention
> Committee, *Inquiry into Public Drunkenness – Final
> Report* (2001).

If repeated reference is made to a particular class of public documents,
for example, reports of parliamentary debates, votes and proceedings,
or parliamentary papers, you can adopt an abbreviated mode of
citation and spell out what the abbreviations mean in a table of
abbreviations.

3.9.2 Parliamentary Papers

Parliamentary papers are documents presented to a parliament that have been ordered to be printed, thus becoming part of a numbered parliamentary papers series. A parliamentary paper should, where possible, be referred to by its number. For example:

> Australia, Parliament, House of Representatives Standing Committee on Legal and Constitutional Affairs, *Cracking Down on Copycats: Enforcement of Copyright in Australia*, Parl Paper No 412 (2000), 47.

> Australia, Parliament, *Central Land Council: Annual Report 1999-2000*, Parl Paper 436 (2000), 58.

The numbers of Commonwealth parliamentary papers can be ascertained by consulting the Indexes to the Papers Presented to Parliament. To the end of 1971, documents which were included in the bound volumes of Commonwealth parliamentary papers carried two series of numbers – one for the particular document and another, stamped, for the volume. Care should be taken to maintain consistency in the page numbers referred to – that of the particular document being discussed.

Many reports and papers included in the bound volumes of parliamentary papers are published and sold separately. In this case, the footnote citation may omit the reference to the relevant volume of the parliamentary papers and identify the report or paper simply by its source, title, date (and number, if it has one). For example:

> Department of Foreign Affairs and Trade, *Annual Report 2000-01* (AusInfo, Canberra, 2001).

3.9.3 Command Papers

The method of citing United Kingdom Command Papers should be noted. For the period 1833-1868/9 only the number of the Paper is cited; from 1870-1899 the number has the prefix 'C'; from 1900-1918, 'Cd'; from 1918-1956/7, 'Cmd'; from 1956/7-1985/6, 'Cmnd'; from 1986/7 to date, 'Cm'. For example:

Great Britain, *Report of the Committee of Privy Councillors Appointed to Inquire into the Interception of Communications* (1957), Cmnd 283.

Great Britain, Law Commission, *Administrative Law: Judicial Review and Statutory Appeals*, Report No 226 (1994), Cm 2646.

3.10 Unpublished Material

3.10.1 Manuscript Collections

This type of material should be described in sufficient detail to enable the reader to locate it and identify it with the least possible effort. If the author or authors of the material have supplied a title, that title should be given in single quotation marks. If the student supplies a title to untitled material, the supplied title is not enclosed in quotation marks.

For manuscript collections, it is essential to cite the location of the material, the title of the collection (if any), the number or numbers (if any) assigned to it by the person or authority holding the material, and, if the material is bound into volumes, the title and number of the volume. For example:

Forbes to Mackaness, 4 July 1825, Supreme Court Letter Book, 44, NSW State Archives, Sydney.

Barron Field to Marsden, 16 December 1824, Marsden Papers, A 3939 (A 23), Mitchell Library, Sydney.

Forbes to Wilmot Horton, 7 March 1826, CO 201/166, PRO, London (in microfilm at National Library).

Manuscript Minutes of Meeting of La Trobe Benevolent Society, vol 62. (These are now located in the Business Archives Section of the Deakin Library in the University of the Riverina.)

If the manuscripts cited are held privately, they should be described with sufficient particularity to enable other researchers, who may later wish to gain access to the collection, to turn them up quickly. This may involve giving a description of the appearance of the material. The date on which the material was consulted should also be indicated. For example:

> Entry for 10 July 1865 in the manuscript Diary of Henderson J for 1 January – 31 December 1865 in the possession (1968) of Mrs Florence Drayton of Prospect, Tasmania. The diary is written in a half-calf volume entitled Ledger Book.

3.10.2 Theses

For theses for higher degrees, the following form of citation should be used:

> Peter L Jenks, 'Manufacturers' Liability in Tort' (unpublished Master of Laws thesis, Law Library, Bass University, 1992), p 72.

3.11 Unwritten Sources: Interviews, Speeches, etc

When citing interviews, talks broadcast by radio or television, public addresses, speeches or lectures, or exchanges of correspondence, use the following general form:

> Interview with John F Smith, Director of the Centre for Community Services, Melbourne, 10 September 2008.

> Lee Gallagher, 'Globalisation of the Music Industry', radio talk broadcast by Triple J, Sydney, 5 May 2003.

> George Anderley, National Director of the US Department of Justice and Home Affairs, personal communication [telephone discussion] with the author, 20 October 2001.

> Australian Broadcasting Corporation, Radio National, The Law Report, 'Australia's Anti-Terrorism Laws', Tuesday 12 February 2002 <http://www.abc.net.au/rn/talks/8.30/lawrpt/stories/s479175.htm> at 14 February 2002.

> Lederman J, *The Application of Taxes to the Food Industry*, Speech 31 May 2001 <http://www.ausfood-

news.com.au/onlinespeech/speech2000/index.htm> at 15 May 2002.

3.12 Second-hand Citations

If the only source available is a secondary one, the fact that a secondary source has been relied upon must be clearly indicated in the citation. One of the following forms should be used:

Davies PL, *The Doctrine of Consideration* (Erewhon Pty Ltd, Sydney, 1954), p 62, citing Finch S, *De Legibus* (Buck House, London, 1615), p 17.

Finch S, *De Legibus* (Buck House, London, 1615), p 17, cited by Davies PL, *The Doctrine of Consideration* (Erewhon Pty Ltd, Sydney, 1954), p 62.

The first form is appropriate where the emphasis is on Davies' citation of Finch; the second form where what Finch wrote is more important that Davies' quoting him.

3.13 Citation of Electronic Material

Material that is available by means of an electronic search *and* in printed form can be cited in either form. Often the electronic search will produce a PDF file which is a printable reproduction version complete with page numbers. Cite these as though they are the actual printed versions. The PDF version should be used in preference to the HTML version. When material is *only* available in electronic form, or when material is more easily accessible electronically (for example, newspaper articles), then sufficient information should be given to enable the reader to identify the material and the means by which it was obtained. Where internet addresses are relied upon in accessing material the reference should include the URL (uniform resource locator) enclosed in angle brackets < > and the date on which it was accessed, eg:

Reynolds R, 'The Four Worlds Theory', *Terra Nova Blog*, 28 August 2005 <http://terranova.blogs.com/ terra_nova/2005/08/the_four_worlds.html> at 18 December 2008.

When citing an article in a newspaper or weekly journal which has been located electronically via an online database, the basic method of citation set out at **3.7 Newspapers or Weekly Journals** above, should be adopted, followed by information indicating the means by which the article may be retrieved and the date it was accessed. For example:

'US Patriot Law Could Involve Local Banks', *Australian Financial Review*, 12 February 2002, p 43, Online LexisNexis at 5 March 2002.

Dworkin R, 'The real threat to US values: The September 11 attacks struck at the heart of America. But emergency measures to combat terrorism could undermine the country's most cherished freedoms', *The Guardian (London)*, 9 March 2002, Saturday Pages, p 3, Online LexisNexis at 20 March 2002.

Where you have accessed the online version of the newspaper, you should cite it as follows:

Beckford M, 'Britons' health at risk from time spent in virtual worlds, says Dr Aric Sigman', *Telegraph.co.uk*, 18 February 2009, <http://www.telegraph.co.uk/health/ healthnews/4688338/Britons-health-at-risk-from-time-spent-in-virtual-worlds-says-Dr-Aric-Sigman.html> at 26 February 2009.

Unreported cases (ones for which the reasons for judgment have never been printed in a law report series) should include the name of the court in which the case was heard, the date on which the decision was handed down and the means by which it may be retrieved:

R v Armanios [1999] NSWDRGC 5 (unreported, Drug Court of New South Wales, Milson J, 12 May 1999) <http://www.austlii.edu.au/au/cases/nsw/ NSWDRGC/1999/5.html> at 2 February 2002.

If a medium neutral citation is available for an as yet unreported case at an appeal court level, it is not essential to indicate exactly how the case was accessed electronically. For instance the case below can be accessed via the official High Court Home Page <http://www. hcourt.gov.au> which provides a link to *AustLII* (Australian Legal

Information Institute – <http://www.austlii.edu.au>), or commercial services such as *LexisNexis AU* and *Legal Online* (your law library will have subscriptions to these services). The following will be sufficient until the case appears in a law report series: *Wurridjal v Commonwealth of Australia* [2009] HCA 2.

If a more complete citation is called for, the names of the judges and the actual date of judgment should be added:

> *Wurridjal v Commonwealth of Australia* [2009] HCA
> 2 (unreported, French CJ, Gummow, Kirby, Hayne,
> Heydon, Crennan and Kiefel JJ, 2 February 2009).

Articles in periodicals which are only published electronically will differ from printed articles in that there will be no page numbers. However the growing convention is to number each paragraph sequentially. The number will be in square brackets [ ]. The details of the article and the electronic journal in which it is published should be followed by all the information necessary for its retrieval, and the date on which it was accessed. For example:

> Cranwell G, 'The Case for Parliamentary Approval of
> Treaties in Australia' (2001) 8(4) *E Law – Murdoch
> University Electronic Journal of Law* <http://www.
> murdoch.edu.au/elaw/indices/issue/v8n4.html> at 11
> April 2002.

In this journal paragraph numbering is used to allow particular passages to be located, eg:

> See Cranwell, n 20 above, at [7].

If paragraph numbering has not been used, a catchword or 'catch phrase' from the relevant part, or the opening words of the relevant paragraph in the material should be given, eg:

> See Cranwell, n 20 above, at heading 'Need for parlia-
> mentary approval'.

> See Cranwell, n 20 above, para beginning 'There are two
> major deficiencies ...'.

For further information about the citation of electronic material, consult Stuhmcke A, *Legal Referencing* (3rd ed, LexisNexis Butterworths, Sydney, 2005).

3.14 Later References

3.14.1 General Rules

> When a source has been cited once in complete form, subsequent references to the same source may be in a shortened form.

However, it is advisable to use the complete form when the citations are widely separated from one another. Thus if there is a footnote reference to Zittrain J, *The Future of the Internet- and how to stop it,* Yale University Press, New Haven & London, 2008, subsequent references, if they are not widely separated, may be in a shortened form, for example, Zittrain, n 2 above, 40, or Zittrain, *The Future of the Internet* p 40.

Case citations are ordinarily so short that, unless the repeating citations follow one another consecutively, the second and subsequent citations should be repeated in full.

The abbreviated Latin terms 'id', 'ibid' (and less frequently 'op cit' and 'loc cit') may be used instead of repeating a citation in full within a chapter, but they are used less often these days. It is now much more common to use a shortened form.

> It is best to use the shortened form when preparing early drafts of a document when text and footnotes are still likely to be moved to some other location because it will not always be clear what 'id' or 'ibid' are referring to and a cross-reference to another footnote number may no longer be valid.

3.14.2 Use of 'Id'

The abbreviation 'id', which stands for 'idem' (meaning 'the same'), is used to repeat the immediately preceding reference without alteration. For example:

2 *Bennett v Bennett* [1952] 1 KB 249 at 260.
3 Id.

> 4   Stone J, *Social Dimensions of Law and Justice*
> (Maitland Publications, Sydney, 1966), p 18.
>
> 5   Id.

'Id' should not be used to repeat a citation when there are intervening footnotes citing other sources or citing the same source but different pages. And 'id' should *never* be used in relation to legislation.

3.14.3   Use of 'Ibid'

The abbreviation 'ibid' stands for 'ibidem' (meaning 'in the same work') and is used to repeat all the immediately preceding citations *except* the page or paragraph numbers, and in the case of a multi-volumed work, the volume and page or paragraph numbers. For example:

> 12   *Re McArdle* [1951] Ch 699 at 671.
>
> 13   Ibid at 674.
>
> 14   Ibid at 676.
>
> 15   Ricketson S, *Intellectual Property: Cases, Materials, and Commentary* (2nd ed, Butterworths, Sydney, 1998), para [11.2.1].
>
> 16   Ibid, para [11.2.4].
>
> 17   Holdsworth WS, 11 *A History of English Law* (Methuen & Co Ltd, Sweet and Maxwell, 1938, reprinted 1966), p 371.
>
> 18   Ibid, 12, p 456.

'Ibid' should *never* be used in relation to legislation.

3.14.4   Use of 'Op Cit'

The abbreviation 'op cit' stands for 'opere citato' (meaning 'in the work cited'). It is used to refer to a work already cited in full form when a different part of that work is cited and when references to other sources have intervened. For example:

> 7   Campbell E and Lee HP, *The Australian Judiciary* (Cambridge University Press, Melbourne, 2001), p 55.

8   *Victoria v Commonwealth* (1926) 38 CLR 399.

9   Campbell and Lee, op cit (n 7), p 103.

The insertion of '(n 7)' is optional. It is, however, helpful to the reader, especially if the first reference to the work is widely separated from the subsequent reference or references.

'Op cit' should *never* be used in relation to legislation or to reports of judicial decisions.

While the use of 'op cit' is permissible, the better mode of citation in cases where 'op cit' is appropriate is as follows:

7   Campbell E and Lee HP, *The Australian Judiciary* (Cambridge University Press, Melbourne, 2001), p 55.

8   *Victoria v Commonwealth* (1926) 38 CLR 399.

9   Campbell and Lee, n 7, p 103.

10   Pannam CL, 'Unconstitutional Statutes and De Facto Officers' (1966) 2 *Federal Law Review* 37.

11   *R v Lisle* (1738) 2 Str 1090 (93 ER 1051).

12   Pannam, n 10, 39.

If more than one work by the same author has been cited, subsequent references to the works of that author should mention the title. If the titles are long they may be shortened.

3.14.5   Use of 'Loc Cit'

The abbreviation 'loc cit' stands for 'loco citato' (meaning 'the place cited'). It is used to repeat the same reference to a work – the same volume and/or page or paragraph as that last cited when citations of other works have intervened. For example:

7   Campbell E and Lee HP, *The Australian Judiciary* (Cambridge University Press, Melbourne, 2001), p 55.

8   *Victoria v Commonwealth* (1926) 38 CLR 399.

9   Campbell and Lee, loc cit.

'Loc cit' should not be used in relation to legislation or to reports of judicial decisions.

LIVERPOOL JOHN MOORES UNIVERSITY
LEARNING SERVICES

While the use of 'loc cit' is permissible, it is suggested that the preferred mode of citation illustrated for 'op cit', at *3.14.4 Use of 'Op Cit'* above, also be adopted for 'loc cit'.

3.15 Cross-references

When cross-referring to other pages or sections of the work, use the words 'above' and 'below' rather than 'supra' and 'infra' or 'ante' and 'post'.

3.16 Quotations in Footnotes and Endnotes

Quotations in footnotes and endnotes should be enclosed by single quotation marks; they need not be indented. Otherwise they should be written in the same way as they would be written in the text. The citation for a quotation in a footnote should be written as follows:

> 6   'The forms of action we have buried, but they still rule us from their graves': Maitland FW, *The Forms of Action at Common Law* (Cambridge University Press, Cambridge, 1936), p 2.

3.17 Indicating the Weight and Significance of Citations

When a citation is used merely to document a quotation or to indicate the authorities or evidence supporting a statement in the text, it needs no introduction or comment. Some explanatory comment is needed when the citation refers to sources which do not directly support propositions in the text, or which are opposed to the views there expressed, or which introduce supplementary material. There are several compendious expressions, English, Latin and Law French, which may be used to indicate the weight and significance of citations. The abbreviated foreign terms have traditionally been italicised, but this is no longer necessary.

'Cf' is the abbreviation for 'confer', the Latin for 'compare'. Either 'compare' or 'cf' may be used to introduce a citation which does not directly support the statement made in the text, but which is not entirely inconsistent with it. If 'cf' is used with reference to a judicial decision, what the writer is suggesting is that the decision is comparable with the decision previously mentioned but is not on all fours. On the other hand, if the citation is introduced with the words 'but cf', what is suggested is that the case cited does not square at all with the case previously mentioned.

'Contra' means 'against' or 'opposing'. It is used to introduce a citation of an authority which is contrary to that previously mentioned.

'Eg' is an abbreviation which stands for 'exempli gratia', meaning 'for the sake of example'. It may be used to introduce a citation of an authority or authorities which are referred to for the purposes of illustration. The use of 'eg' indicates that what follows is not exhaustive. ('See' or 'See eg' may be used to the same effect. 'See' is preferable to 'vide'.)

The abbreviation 'ie' stands for 'id est', meaning 'that is', and is used to introduce an explanation or definition.

The words 'but see' should be used to introduce citation of an authority which, though not opposed to the conclusion the writer has reached, is not entirely consistent with it.

'Semble' is a Law French word meaning 'it seems' or 'it seems that'. It is used to preface a debatable interpretation of legislation or a judicial decision or pronouncement.

'Per' is a Latin word meaning 'by', and is used in the following way:

> *Banbury v Bank of Montreal* [1918] AC 626 at 657 per Lord Finlay LC.

3.18 Abbreviations and Contractions in Notes

Abbreviations and contractions may be used in footnotes and endnotes even where their use in the text is not permissible. The following lists set out those abbreviations likely to occur most often. Abbreviations for series of law reports and for legal periodicals are not included; for these, see the publications listed at **3.5 Cases** above.

3.18.1 Sovereigns

The following abbreviations for sovereigns should be used when citing statutes by regnal years:

Car	Charles
Edw	Edward
Eliz	Elizabeth
Geo	George
Hen	Henry
Jac	James
M	Mary
Ph & M	Philip and Mary
Ric	Richard
Vic or Vict	Victoria (following the abbreviation used in the relevant statute book)
Will	William
Will & M	William and Mary

3.18.2 Courts

If the name of the court is added after a case citation, use the following abbreviations:

Adm	Admiralty Court or Division
CA	Court of Appeal
CCA	Court of Criminal Appeal
Ch	Chancery Court or Division
CP	Common Pleas Court or Division
Dist Ct	District Court
Div Ct	Divisional Court
Eq	Equity Court or Division
Ex	Exchequer Court or Division
Fam Ct	Family Court
Fed Ct	Federal Court
FMS	Federal Magistrates' Service
Full Ct	Full Court
High Ct or HC	High Court
HL	House of Lords
ICC	International Criminal Court
ICJ	International Court of Justice
Ind Ct	Industrial Court
KB	King's Bench or Division
PC	Judicial Committee of the Privy Council

QB	Queen's Bench or Division
Q Sess	Quarter Sessions
Sup Ct or SC	Supreme Court

3.18.3 Countries and States

The following are standard abbreviations for some countries, the Australian States and the Territories of the Commonwealth of Australia:

ACT	Australian Capital Territory
Aust	Australia
Can	Canada
Cth	Commonwealth of Australia
Eng	England
Gt Brit	Great Britain
Ir (before 1922)	Ireland
Ir Rep	Irish Republic
NI	Northern Ireland
NSW	New South Wales
NT	Northern Territory
NZ	New Zealand
PNG	Papua New Guinea
Qld	Queensland
SA	South Australia
S Af	South Africa
Scot	Scotland
Tas	Tasmania
UK	United Kingdom
USA	United States of America
Vic	Victoria
WA	Western Australia

3.18.4 Legislative Institutions

Legislative institutions are abbreviated as follows:

HA	House of Assembly
HC	House of Commons
HL	House of Lords
HR	House of Representatives
LA	Legislative Assembly
LC	Legislative Council
Sen or S	Senate

3.18.5   Other Bodies and Agencies

The following are examples of abbreviations and contractions for some other bodies and agencies:

AAT	Administrative Appeals Tribunal
ABC	Australian Broadcasting Corporation
ACC	Australian Crime Commission
ACCC	Australian Competition and Consumer Commission
AFP	Australian Federal Police
AGPS	Australian Government Publishing Service
AHRC	Australian Human Rights Commission
ALRC	Australian Law Reform Commission
ARC	Administrative Review Council
ASIC	Australian Securities and Investments Commission
ASIO	Australian Security Intelligence Organisation
ATO	Australian Taxation Office
AUSTEL	Australian Telecommunications Authority
Assn	Association
Bd	Board
Bros	Brothers
Co	Company
Co-op	Co-operative
Corp	Corporation
Dept	Department
EEC	European Economic Community (now the European Union (EU))
Fedn	Federation
Govt	Government
Inc	Incorporated
ILO	International Labour Organisation
Ltd	Limited
NGO	Non-government organisation
plc	public limited company
Pty	Proprietary
UN	United Nations
WHO	World Health Organisation

3.18.6   Officials

Official titles are abbreviated or contracted as follows:

ACJ	Acting Chief Justice
A-G	Attorney-General

AJ	Acting Judge or Justice
A-JA	Acting Judge of Appeal
B	Baron (Exchequer)
CB	Chief Baron (Exchequer)
CFM	Chief Federal Magistrate
CJ	Chief Justice or Chief Judge
CJ in Eq	Chief Judge in Equity
Commr	Commissioner
DPP	Director of Public Prosecutions
FCT	Federal Commissioner of Taxation
FM	Federal Magistrate
Gov	Governor
Gov-Gen	Governor-General
J	Justice or Judge
JA	Judge of Appeal
JJ	Justices
JJA	Judges of Appeal
LC	Lord Chancellor
LCB	Lord Chief Baron (Exchequer)
LCJ	Lord Chief Justice
LJ	Lord Justice
MR	Master of the Rolls
P	President (of a court)
QC	Queen's Counsel
SC	Senior Counsel
SM	Stipendiary Magistrate
Sol-Gen	Solicitor-General
SPJ	Senior Puisne Judge
VC	Vice-Chancellor

3.18.7 Miscellaneous

The following are abbreviations of miscellaneous English and Latin words, some of which have been mentioned previously:

anon	anonymous
art, arts	article(s)
c or ca	about (Latin 'circa'). (Used when an exact date cannot be determined.)
cf	compare (Latin 'confer')
cap	heading, chapter (Latin 'capite')
chap, chaps	chapter(s)
cl, cll	clause(s)

col, cols	column(s)
div, divs	division(s)
ed, eds, edn	editor(s), edited by, edition
eg	for example (Latin 'exempli gratia')
et al	and others (Latin 'et alii'). (Used when a book has several authors, eg J Smith et al.)
et seq	and following (Latin 'et sequentes'). (One or more pages following that indicated, but where possible precise page references should be given, eg, pp 150-158.)
ex parte	on the part of one side only; on behalf of
ex rel	on relation or information (Latin 'ex relatione')
ibid	ibid in the same work (Latin 'ibidem')
id	the same (Latin 'idem')
ie	that is (Latin 'id est')
infra	below (Latin 'infra'). (Used to indicate discussion to follow, but the word 'below' is preferred.)
loc cit	in the place cited (Latin 'loco citato')
ms, mss	manuscript(s)
nd	no date. (Used when the date of publication is not given.)
n, nn	note(s)
NS	New Series. (Used in some law reports and periodicals
nv	we have not seen (Latin 'non vidimus')
op cit	in the work cited (Latin 'opere citato')
p, pp	page(s)
para, paras	paragraph(s)
passim	in various places
pseud	pseudonym
pt, pts	part(s)
qv	which see (Latin 'quod vide')
repr	reprint, reprinted
rev	revised
sub nom	under the name (Latin 'sub nomine')
supra	above (Latin 'supra'). (Used to indicate previous discussion, but 'above' is preferred.)
tr, trans	translated by, translator(s)
vide	see (Latin 'vide')
v	against (Latin 'versus')
vol, vols	volume(s)

3.19 Position and Spacing of Notes

Footnotes positioned at the bottom of the page should begin four line spaces below the last line of the text. Each footnote should be single-spaced, with one and a half spaces between each succeeding footnote. They may be continued from page to page but this is to be avoided as far as possible.

The footnote number should be aligned with the margin (no full stop is necessary), and the footnote itself should start two letter spaces from the number, creating a margin for the rest of the footnote. For example:

> 98 See, for example, *R v Geesing* (1985) 38 SASR 226, which involves threats to fellow prisoners.

3.20 Numbering of Notes

Footnotes should be numbered continuously throughout and not numbered afresh on each page. Endnotes should also be numbered continuously for the entire work.

The footnote and endnote indicators in the text should not be printed in parenthesis nor in italics. A note indicator should stand at the end of a clause or sentence, or after the word or title concerned, and at the end of a quotation. It should follow, not precede, punctuation marks. For example:

> In the case of *Smith v Brown*,[4] decided in 1944, ...

> As White J pointed out in *Smith v Brown*, there is no obligation to ... purchaser.[5]

> In *Smith v Brown*, White J concluded that 'although there is no obligation to ... vendor'.[6]

If it is necessary to add notes after the work has been completed and a word processor is not being used, then the additions should be numbered thus: 18a, 18b etc.

PART 4
Approaching Law Exams

4.1   Pre-exam Preparation

4.1.1   Keeping Up With Reading and Attending Lectures

In theory, all you need to do at exam time is to bring your reviewing of class material and readings up to date in each subject. Your exam preparation will involve surveying the whole subject (or those parts of it subject to examination), but the component parts of it should have been brought up to date as the subject proceeded. Increasingly universities are responding to student demand for flexible learning and provide recordings of lectures online. Whilst this is an excellent resource for students who are ill or have a timetable clash, it is important that students do not come to rely on listening to these recordings as a substitute for more focused study. Listening to recordings more than once is not necessary.

> You should treat such recordings as you would a face-to-face lecture, which you attend and take notes. You should listen to lectures as soon as possible after the class so that you are able to keep in synch with the coverage of materials in class and where relevant, tutorials in that unit. Where possible you should attend lectures as this will give you an opportunity to ask the lecturer questions to clarify the material, to meet other students and to keep up to date with reading. Further, you should not rely solely on recorded lectures.
>
> Common problems created by over-reliance on recorded lectures are failure to reference cases and others sources correctly where you rely on the aural cues. Misspelt case names are a clear indication that you have not done any reading, and show a lack of depth to your answer. Finally, a reference to a lecturer and lecture date is not sufficient authority to support a legal argument, you must refer to the relevant legislation, case, or other official source.

Further, if you intend to listen to recordings of classes for the first time in the last few days before the exam and develop an understanding of the whole unit, you will find that you do not have time to sufficiently absorb and understand key concepts. Nor will you have time in the exam to revisit lengthy notes.

> *If you think that you will have time to bring scattered lecture notes up to date and complete the reading of the additional references and will be able to consolidate all the material into a coherent whole between the end of lectures and the beginning of the exams, you will be in trouble.*

4.1.2   Preparing Outlines

Your notes should bring together the structure of the subject as outlined in lectures together with your supplementary reading so as to produce a systematic view of the law which identifies issues, states rules or, where the rules are not clear, spells out the nature of the conflicts and their possible resolution according to authority, principle or policy. You may also find it useful to prepare a checklist of issues for each topic. Your notes should not only reflect an understanding of the law, but also its underlying policies, for example allocation of risks and losses, priority of certain values such as privacy, or balancing competing interests, for example quality of life versus sanctity of life.

4.1.3   Periodic Review

When your notes and materials on each major part of the course are completed and summarised, you should review the overall structure in an effort to place the topic in its proper context within the subject. Many students have a problem placing topics in perspective and seeing parallels and links between one area and another. Remember the law often develops by analogy, and the judges frequently seek to enunciate the underlying principles which serve to integrate and simplify related areas of law, as in the evolution of the law of manslaughter. Awareness of possible analogies and parallels makes for better grades.

4.1.4   Practice Previous Exams

Better students attempt previous exam questions. This opportunity should be available to you in tutorials, but if not, form your own study group. Copies of previous examination papers are usually available in the library, or the web page associated with the particular subject. Past exam questions with sample solutions can be found in Krever R, *Mastering Law Studies and Law Exam Techniques* (6th ed, LexisNexis Butterworths, Sydney, 2006), Ch 9. Beware – the course content may have changed significantly in just a few years, making some questions and answers less useful.

> *Practise answering the questions in the time allocated. Learn to make best use of the time available.*

4.1.5   Developing an Exam Room Technique

When working on practice exam questions, attempt the question in exam conditions and allot yourself the same time for reading and writing as you would have in the examination room. Effective time allocation in an exam is critical to success.

4.1.6   Form a Study Group

You will improve your legal knowledge and technique if you form or join a study group of about four or five students to meet regularly to discuss the material being taught and to provide mutual help and feedback on solving problems. All learning benefits from discussion with others. If you are having difficulty establishing a study group, ask your lecturer or tutor to use some class time to announce that there is an interest in setting up such groups and to facilitate their formation. Use the study group as a vehicle for attempting past exam questions. All agree to prepare an answer at home under exam conditions (including time limits) and bring the answer to the next study group meeting. Exchange answers and discuss what issues were raised by the problem. Grade each other's work.

4.2 Types of Exam

4.2.1 Multiple Choice 'Objective' Examinations

These embody 'true/false' statements, or 'multiple choice' propositions, which require the selection of a 'correct', or 'nearest correct' answer. They tend to be used as a form of continuing assessment rather than for final examinations because they are largely designed to provide a check on your progress and to determine whether you have acquired basic information in the subject. They do not involve the type of problem solving that characterises the final exam, but they do require knowledge of the underlying principles and a fair amount of the detail of the law being examined. In this type of exam, be realistic about whether it is worthwhile looking up answers to those questions about which you are unsure rather than going on to respond to the items to which you do know the answer. Because there will be many questions (you will be told how many in advance) pacing yourself through the exam to make best use of the available time is very important.

4.2.2 Problem Type

This is the most common type of law exam question. It usually consists of a description of a factual situation (or variations of a factual situation) which give rise to legal issues that require some sort of decision or advice. Such questions test your abilities as a lawyer because their aim is to present you with the type of legal problem that is faced in practice and in the courts. In framing the question, it is common for examiners not to give students any clue regarding the legal issues being raised. You have to extract them from the facts. This means that you will need to understand both the broad legal classifications which might be applicable, and you must also possess specific knowledge within those areas to be able to address the detailed legal points raised by the question.

Problem questions are deliberately designed by examiners to raise multiple issues and ones for which the law does not currently provide a clear answer. This means that your initial reaction of not knowing the answer is quite legitimate. These problems must be understood to be similar to those in mathematics. Not to know the answer immediately in mathematics is not regarded as a fault, provided that the person can reach a solution by using appropriate mathematical symbols and formulae. So too in law, but instead of applying mathematical symbols and rules, the language of the law is used to provide the symbols and rules of analysis. As in mathematics, you should only expect to reach the conclusion at the end of the answer, not at the beginning.

This is not to say that you cannot open your response by indicating what you consider to be the main issues raised by the problem. However, unlike research assignments and other exercises in which you have time to prepare successive drafts and can present your considered conclusions as an opening statement, the pressure of the exam setting makes it wiser to postpone your conclusions until you have actually arrived at them in a considered fashion.

4.2.3   Essay or Policy Type

The essay or policy type question as posed in law exams often raises issues similar to those in a problem type question, but is less constrained by a particular set of facts. Examiners will not ask questions like 'What is the law of libel in this State?', which only require an exposition of the current law. Instead, they pose questions which call for you to take a position on areas of uncertainty of the law, or on aspects which test the boundaries of the law, for instance whether some of the new electronic forms of communication can fit readily into the existing law of defamation or whether the existing law is capable of being extended to recognise new rights or defences. Essay type questions invariably call for you to comment on, or agree or disagree with, a particular proposition. Understand that, in responding to that proposition, you are being invited to demonstrate both familiarity with the particular area of law and the competing policies behind it. You must critically address the specific aspect raised by the question and not some other one which has not been asked. And you must clearly indicate what your views are on the policy points. In doing so it is to your advantage to cite cases or other sources which lend support to your position.

> *It is dangerous to rely on prepared answers to policy questions – do not fall into the trap of answering a question that you hoped would be on the paper, rather than the one that is actually on the paper. Writing generally on the topic is no substitute for answering the question.*

4.2.4   Open Book, Closed Book, Take-Home Exams

You should inform yourself regarding the nature and format of the exam. Most law exams these days are 'Open Book' because they are more concerned with testing your understanding and application of principles of law than simply expecting rote learning and regurgitation. Closed book exams may take the form of shorter class tests, revision exercises, true/false and short answer questions, or may be in the same format as longer open book exams. In this case materials such as case lists and extracts from legislation may be provided in the exam room. It is therefore essential that you are certain what type of exam you are facing, what materials you are permitted to bring into the exam and what you may expect to be provided with in the exam room. The 'Open Book' examination appears advantageous because students can bring their personal notes or books into the examination room for consultation in the course of the exam. Students who are ill prepared are warned that, in a time limited 'Open Book' exam they are unlikely to have time to consult the material they are permitted to take into the exam room. The notes provide a 'security blanket' but there is no time to start learning material for the first time. It becomes even more dangerous to bring notes with prepared passages the student thinks might be relevant to questions in the exam paper and to copy them in without discrimination or critical application to the question asked.

'Take-home' exams are ones in which students enrolled in subjects which have a strong research emphasis are assigned a problem for which they are allowed 24 hours or a longer period, such as a weekend, in which to undertake research and to prepare a written response. Word limits apply and it is not uncommon for students to be permitted to utilise the law library during that period. These are challenging exercises, but as with all forms of examination a good understanding of the subject matter of the course in which the examination is set and practise in developing systematic approaches to research and writing will produce good results. Because the time-frame for completion of the assessable exercise is longer, it is highly desirable that time be allowed for the paper to be completed and then critically reviewed and revised by the student prior to being submitted.

4.3 What the Examiners are Looking For

4.3.1 Differences Between Examiners

It is unlikely that any two examiners will be in complete agreement about what constitutes a perfect answer to a problem question. But this is not the nature of the examining process. Examiners are not looking for a perfect answer, they are looking to see how completely a candidate can identify and analyse issues which are raised in the question. Discrepancies between examiners and between streams are controlled in a number of ways. These include the circulation and analysis of questions prior to their being included in the paper; the preparation of checklists for individual examiners in which the balance of marks between different components of the paper are set out (whilst still leaving some discretionary marks for different styles and unexpected quality); the second grading of all fail and top grade students and, amongst most examiners, a review of students sitting on the border between one grade and a higher one. In multi-stream subjects, each student is ordinarily assessed by reference to the performance of all students enrolled in the subject, not just those in the same stream.

4.3.2 An Answer to the Question

Your answer is expected to be an answer. When you are given a set of facts and a question about them you are expected to answer the question that is asked. Neither the problems nor the essay questions are made up merely to give you an opportunity to regurgitate all the rules and cases you can think of. The examiner wants a response to a particular problem, just as the client wants a solution to a specific problem. And the answer must be supported by reasons. In effect you are being asked for a concise legal opinion similar to those handed down by the courts. You are to explain why you think the law requires the particular decision you have reached. You will have to be able to identify the multiple legal issues raised by the problem – both the primary heads of liability and the subsidiary issues within each head (and these may differ if there are multiple parties); the relevant law (examining the position both for and against your client's interest); and the application of the law to the facts. The answer must then end with the advice or conclusion asked for. This may involve facing a 'too hard' problem, but you should nevertheless state the difficulties and try to resolve them in terms of the policies which underpin the law and indicate why you regard the particular result the best that the client can achieve. Your answer should be well structured, with evidence of planning; headings should be used.

4.3.3   Grades

The grading system and the numerical values that delimit each level may differ between institutions. However the qualities expected for the higher level grades can be described in terms similar to those set out below:

Fail:
An unsatisfactory level of achievement in relation to the assessable tasks. The candidate has not addressed sufficiently the legal issues raised by the task and/or does not understand the relevant law. He or she has failed to make any serious attempt to deal with the issues which have been identified, or has done so in a grossly inadequate fashion.

Pass:
A satisfactory level of achievement in relation to the assessable tasks. The candidate has identified the principal issues, and generally applies the law accurately, but does not explore them

in any detail and leaves difficulties unexamined. Alternatively, he or she may have addressed some issues quite well, but omitted others or mentioned them quite briefly. In the upper Pass range, the candidate may have attempted a more detailed examination of the relevant law, but has not supplied sufficient reasoning and authority to justify the conclusions.

Credit:

A better level of achievement in relation to the assessable tasks. The candidate demonstrates a more reasoned explanation for the conclusions reached and the citation of authority indicates better familiarity with the relevant cases and legislation.

Distinction:

A high level of achievement in relation to the assessable tasks. All significant legal issues have been raised by the candidate and reasoned conclusions presented. The main positions likely to be taken by either side are identified and the candidate's responses show evidence of wider reading and a deeper under-standing of the complexity of the case law, legislation and underlying policy.

High Distinction:

An excellent level of achievement in relation to the assessable tasks. The candidate's response reveals evidence of a deeper understanding of the complexities of the issues. Relevant indi-cators include: ability to identify the position likely to be taken by each side; presentation of reasoned conclusions; citation of authority which reveals familiarity with relevant cases and legislation; support of those conclusions by evidence of wider reading; and a willingness to offer proposals for resolution of the problem, or reform of the relevant law.

In general, anyone who is prepared for the exam should be able to pass because one-third of the available grade is earned for identifying the issues raised by the problem; one-third for citing relevant legisla-tion and cases and commenting on the issues; and the final one-third is earned by the superior quality of the arguments presented and the evidence of wider reading.

4.4   On the Way to the Exam

4.4.1   Confirm Dates, Times and Locations

In multi-stream subjects it is important to know what stream you are in to ensure that you attend the appropriate location for your stream. In checking the examination timetable, make sure you are referring to the *final* one.

4.4.2   Instructions and Materials

Bring your ID card to the exam. Before entering the examination room make sure you know whether it is to be an open or closed book exam. If the former, familiarise yourself with the pre-exam instructions given by the lecturer regarding the materials that can be taken into the exam and the number and type of questions to be asked. Work out, in advance, your timing of each question or part.

4.4.3   Notes, Acts and Books

Take into the exam any notes, Acts and books which are permitted. Take spare writing instruments. The books will not help you, but may serve as a security blanket. Your notes will help as a checklist of areas to be covered and you will need to make reference to Acts if the course relies heavily on legislation.

4.4.4   Emergencies, Illness, etc

If, on the way to the examination, you are delayed by an accident or emergency, or some other untoward circumstances, present yourself to the supervisor at the exam room, ask to be allowed to start the exam. Communicate with your lecturer immediately afterwards in any event. If you become ill in the exam and are unable to continue, the examination room supervisor will report that fact to the faculty, but it is important that you also contact your lecturer as soon as possible to tell them what has happened. An application for special consideration or a deferred exam should be lodged following any such emergency or sudden illness.

4.4.5   Application for Special Consideration or Deferred Exam

If your work during a teaching period, or your performance in an examination or other form of assessment, has been significantly affected by illness or other serious cause, your university may permit you to apply for special consideration by the examiners of the subjects in which you are enrolled or to apply for a deferred exam. Applications for special consideration or deferred exam usually have to be submitted on special forms available for this purpose and be accompanied by appropriate medical or other evidence. It is preferable that they be lodged, where possible, prior to the relevant examination and, in any event, within any time limits set by your university.

4.5   In the Examination Room

4.5.1   Pre-examination Anxiety

This is normal and can be dealt with constructively by applying the suggestions which follow.

4.5.2   Timing

This should be worked out before starting to write. Apportion both your reading time and writing time according to the value allocated to each question.

> *Pace yourself so as to stay on this schedule. Write concisely and to the point in order to adhere to this time frame. This is very important; more students get into difficulty by running out of time, or by stealing time from one question to complete an answer to another than through ignorance or error in their legal analysis of the problem. You cannot gain any marks for a question that you have not attempted. Most fail students fail because they do not attempt all required parts of the exam paper. You cannot get more than 40 marks for a question worth 40, no matter how good your answer is!*

4.5.3   Read the Paper as a Whole

Confirm what has to be done in terms of the number of questions to be answered and whether choices are required to be made between the questions and parts of questions. Do not make the mistake of answering all parts of the question when the instructions make it clear that no more than a certain number are to be answered.

4.5.4   Systematic Reading

Divide the available reading time among the available questions. Use the reading time to get the facts clear, to highlight the issues raised (do not attempt to draft answers at this stage), and to resolve choices amongst questions. It is helpful to use the reading time to consider each of the choice options and to decide which one will be attempted. Think carefully about what is involved in any policy or essay questions. Having made a considered choice do not go back on it. Think about how you will structure each question you intend to attempt.

4.5.5   Answering a Question

- Master the facts and the nature of the question asked. If there is more than one party to the proceedings, understand what the relative roles of each are and in relation to whom you are being asked to answer. Go through the facts of the questions slowly and thoroughly; if necessary do so a second time. Try to visualise the situation. Draw a diagram if the facts are complicated. Be sure you haven't misread what is stated in the problem or misunderstood the question. Do not assume facts that are neither stated nor inferable from those that are.

- Identify issues and plan how to approach them in a logical order. Draft a very brief outline of your plan (the main headings and some subheadings will do). Your own checklist will fill in the fine detail.

- Use the headings and subheadings as you write in order to present the answer in a logical manner. These may take the form of questions, for example Did V consent? Was the consent 'free and informed'?

- Write succinctly. Do not write out citations or lengthy quotes in full. Underline case names and statute names. You can use abbreviations such as TPA for *Trade Practices Act 1974* (Cth). But beware, writing out a case name or giving a legislative reference is not a substitute for explaining and applying the legal principle for which it is being utilised.

- State both sides of the legal argument even though you will be emphasising one side in preference to the other. Show that you know there is an opposing view.

- Refer, if necessary, to any additional problems that arise in respect of burden of proof, evidence or matters that relate to the respective roles of judge and jury.

- Do not jump to conclusions nor answer the question on the basis of there being only one significant issue.

- If the facts do not fit and you need more information, mention the fact briefly, but do not labour the point. Explain how that information would assist or alter your conclusions.

- Write coherently. Do not just spray the paper with unconnected sentences and paragraphs and then try to organise them later by rewriting, crossing out, interlineating and inserting arrows. Follow the logical sequence in which the various issues you intend to discuss are connected to one another. Discuss them in that order.

> *One or two minutes spent in organising may save you 10 minutes wasted in writing a page on an aspect that is not relevant.*

- Remember you are building a structure of ideas for someone else to examine. It will be better understood if the basic propositions that form the foundation are clear. That is why headings, subheadings and underlining are so important.

- Remember the examiner is not a mindreader. He or she has not been with you while you analyse the problem and does not know how much or how little you know about it. The examiner does not assume that you know the answer or can solve the problem until you demonstrate that you can. Consequently, in discussing each issue, you should indicate what it is and why it has to be considered. If a matter appears to be only marginally relevant, or seems self-evident, it is worth making that point rather than ignoring it altogether and possibly being wrong about its significance. At least the examiner knows that you did turn your mind to it although you may have reached a wrong conclusion. You get marks for what is on the paper, not what is still in your mind.

- In an emergency you may drop back to answering in the form of an outline with headings and subheadings, but this should not be the principal form of writing. There is no point in writing 'time' as an explanation for not finishing a question. That is a message for yourself.

- Legibility is also important. If your answer is not readable by your examiner, the paper is likely to be graded as a fail. The examiner is not an expert in deciphering secret codes, curious acronyms or gibberish. Writing should be legible and intelligible and you should strive to observe the usual rules of grammar, punctuation and spelling.

- Ensure that each question is clearly preceded by its number or part and that you have written your ID number and name on the front of each examination script book used.

4.6 How to Approach Law Exams?

In a nutshell – preparedly, systematically and confidently.

PART 5
Selected Bibliography

5.1 Guides to Writing Essays and Assignments

Anderson J and Poole M, *Assignment and Thesis Writing* (4th ed, Wiley, Brisbane, 2001).

Clanchy J and Ballard B, *Essay Writing for Students: A Practical Guide* (3rd ed, Addison Wesley Longman, Melbourne, 1997).

Enright C, *Legal Technique* (The Federation Press, Sydney, 2002), Ch 43.

Hutchinson T, *Researching and Writing in Law* (2nd ed, Lawbook Co, Sydney, 2006).

Meehan M and Tulloch G, *Grammar for Lawyers* (2nd ed, Butterworths, Sydney, 2007).

Packham G, McEvedy M and Smith P, *Writing Assignments* (Nelson, Melbourne, 1992).

Rao V, Chanock K and Krishnan L, *A Visual Guide to Essay Writing* (Association for Academic Language and Learning, Sydney, 2007) (available free on the internet as an e-book at: <http://dspace.anu.edu.au/bitstream/1885/47101/1/essay%20writing.pdf>).

Wojcik M, *Introduction to Legal English: An introduction to legal terminology, reasoning and writing in plain English* (2nd ed, International Law Institute, DC, 2001).

5.2 Style Guides (non legal)

Commonwealth of Australia, *Style Manual for Authors, Editors and Printers* (6th ed, Wiley, Milton, Qld, 2002). The full text is available at <http://www.dcita.gov.au/infoaccess/style_manual.html>.

Peters P, *The Cambridge Guide to Australian English Usage* (2nd ed, Cambridge University Press, Port Melbourne, Victoria, 2007).

5.3 Research Guides

Banks C and Douglas H, *Law on the Internet* (3rd ed, The Federation Press, Sydney, 2006).

Bott B, Cowley J and Falconer L, *Nemes and Coss' Effective Legal Research* (3rd ed, LexisNexis Butterworths, Sydney, 2007).

Campbell E, Poh-York L and Tooher J, *Legal Research: Materials and Methods* (4th ed, Law Book Co, Sydney, 1996).

Cook C et al, *Laying Down the Law* (7th ed, LexisNexis Butterworths, Sydney, 2009).

Milne S and Tucker K, *A Practical Guide to Legal Research* (Lawbook, Sydney, 2008).

Watt R, *Concise Legal Research* (6th ed, The Federation Press, Sydney, 2009).

5.4 Citation Guides

Abbreviations of Legal Publications (Monash University Law Library, Melbourne, Updated 2006) Full text version available at <http://www.lib.monash.edu.au/law/abbrevlist/>.

Association of Legal Writing Directors, *ALWD Citation Manual: A Professional System of Citation* (2nd ed, Aspen Law and Business, New York, Garthensburg, 2003). For USA legal citations. Part 4 is devoted to electronic sources and medium neutral citations.

Melbourne University Law Review Association, *Australian Guide to Legal Citation* (2nd ed, Melbourne University Law Review Association, 2002 Melbourne). Full text available at <http://mulr.law.unimelb.edu.au/files/aglcdl.pdf>.

Prince M, *Prince's Dictionary of Legal Citations: A Reference Guide for Attorneys, Legal Secretaries, Paralegals and Law Students* (7th ed, William S Hein, Buffalo, New York, 2006).

Raistrick D, *Index to Legal Citations and Abbreviations* (3rd ed, Sweet & Maxwell, London, 2008).

Stuhmcke A, *Legal Referencing* (3rd ed, LexisNexis Butterworths, Sydney, 2005).

5.5 Exam Guides

Hay I, Bochner D and Dungey C, *Making the Grade* (3rd ed, Oxford University Press, Melbourne, 2006), Ch 16.

Krever R, *Mastering Law Studies and Exam Techniques* (6th ed, Butterworths, Sydney, 2006). Chapter 9 has a sample set of examination questions and answers in various fields.

Stuhmcke A, *Legal Referencing* (3rd ed, LexisNexis Butterworths, Sydney, 2005). Chapter 13 has advice on how to reference sources in exams.

PART 6
Self Assessment

6.1   Self Assessment of Research Skills

Tick the skills you have mastered by the end of first year. You should have acquired the ability to:

> √   *Use legal dictionaries in print or electronic form to find the meaning of legal words and phrases.*
>
> √   *Locate relevant texts and loose-leaf services on a topic of law.*
>
> √   *Use a legal encyclopaedia to gain an initial understanding of, and find legal authorities relating to, a legal principle.*
>
> √   *Find journal articles and case notes on a particular topic using Australian databases such as AGIS, APAIS and Casebase.*
>
> √   *Locate the full text of a journal article, electronically or in print.*
>
> √   *Distinguish between (and be able to locate) sessional and reprinted legislation (the latter incorporates amendments up to the date of reprinting).*
>
> √   *Find Commonwealth and State legislation in print and electronically using sites such as AustLII, Lawlex or ComLaw and via the legislative and parliamentary documents internet pages of Federal and State parliaments.*
>
> √   *Find parliamentary documents associated with a piece of legislation, such as Bills, explanatory memoranda, second reading speeches, government reports, etc.*
>
> √   *Check whether a particular version of an Act is the most current one and update it using print and electronic tools such as the Statutes Annotations, Australian Current Law and Australian Legal Monthly Digest (ALMD) or Lawlex.*

√ *Find commencement information for an Act.*

√ *Find cases on a particular topic using print tools such as Australian Digest, or electronic tools such as Casebase and FirstPoint.*

√ *Find cases in which judicial consideration has been given to particular legislation.*

√ *Find a law report citation for a named party in a case using print and electronic tools such as Australian Case Citator (or FirstPoint) and Casebase.*

√ *Find the full titles of abbreviations for law reports and journals.*

√ *Know the authorised law reports for Australian and UK courts.*

√ *Find the full text of judgments in published law reports, and electronically via services such as AustLII and publisher databases such as LexisNexisAU and Legal Online.*

√ *'Note-up' (or find subsequent references to) a case using databases such as Casebase and FirstPoint.*

6.2   What Type of Student are You?

At the end of their law studies, successful students will not only have completed all exams and research assignments at a high level and in minimum time, but also will have acquired a well-developed set of research, analytical and communication skills as the basis of their future problem solving. They will be aware of the importance of cross-cultural sensitivity and adherence to high ethical standards in their delivery of professional services, equipping them to join the ranks of the legal profession.

Struggling students may have successfully passed all subjects required for their law degree, but their record will be marred by low grades and the need to repeat units. Their research skills will be underdeveloped and their approach to law will be mechanistic and literal, rather than creative and innovative. They will see law as a job rather than a career.

Now that you have reached the end of the book and have prepared and submitted written assignments and sat law exams in your first year, use the table below to evaluate the type of student you are and what more you need to do to get the most out of your law studies and the larger opportunities for personal development in a university setting.

6.3 Successful or Struggling Student?

Successful Student	Struggling Student
Time Management:	*Time Management:*
Thinks about it and uses it. Uses diary or calendar for planning steps in preparing assignments. Each day sets aside some time for study, compilation of notes and revision. During the course of the week tries to spend some time on each subject. Might not be meeting planned goals, but knows what they are and is still trying.	What is that? Diary is in a mess. Procrastinates a lot. Hands in first draft of assessable work. Crams for exams at the last minute. May have got away with it in the past and thinks that law is the same. Is so overwhelmed with the work and so easily distracted, that things are put off even further. Spends a lot of time chatting and running around.
Study Techniques:	*Study Techniques:*
Does more than just read the cases and legislation and take notes. Tries to answer questions posed in the books, reading materials or class. Tries to listen in class and asks: 'Why is the teacher asking these questions?'; 'Where is this all going?' Tries to fit the particular topic into the larger framework of the course. When in trouble, looks beyond prescribed text to other sources in recommended readings and actively seeks help from the teacher, tutors or others.	Stopped reading cases and legislation about half way through the semester. Borrows other students' notes or relies on commercially sold outlines or summaries of legal subjects. Misses many classes and, even when attending, does not really listen because, having not read the prescribed materials, it all seems so pointless. Thinks that memorising is the same as understanding. Does not know how the components of each subject all fit together. When in trouble retreats into a shell.

Successful Student	Struggling Student
Analysing Cases:	*Analysing Cases:*
Reads the judgment as well as the headnote. Tries to work out why the case is in the required reading and how it relates to solving a particular problem or issue. Does not focus so much on the answer arrived at, but rather on setting out how the court got to that result. Reveals the two sides to the problem, as well as the resolution. Is interested in the reasoning behind any dissenting judgment.	Takes short-cuts. Relies on the headnote. Content to underline or highlight what are thought to be important sentences or paragraphs. Finds the idea of analysing or summarising a judgment too much effort. Thinks that if you know what the final result was, it does not matter how the court arrived at its decision. Is not interested in dissenting judgments. Relies on secondary sources rather than reading cases.
Response to Questions in Class:	*Response to Questions in Class:*
Understands that the point of class questioning is not the answer, but how you get there. Realises that responding to questions is designed to develop skills in critical thinking. Understands that Law School is not really about the professor telling you what the law is, but is about discovering how to analyse issues for yourself. Can see the point in arguing by analogy or drawing on dissenting judgments for different solutions.	Cannot cope with the apparent lack of clear answers to legal problems. Regards the grilling of students as pointless. Regards this form of teaching as designed to harass the student rather than help. Wonders why students have to pay fees to teach themselves the law. Prefers to be absent from class and tries to rely on recorded lectures even though they do not pick up the dialogue or discussion with students in class.
Involvement in the Student Community:	*Involvement in the Student Community:*
Regards contact in class and elsewhere as an opportunity to meet other students in order both to socialise and to study and talk over issues and questions. Understands that discussion helps clear things up. Responds to the opportunity to set up study groups with people in the same class or in the same year.	Is not prepared to take the risk of talking to someone else in class; reluctant to reveal ignorance (though half aware that other students also do not know that much either); regards law as a competitive rat race – dog eat dog. Not a member of any study group.

Successful Student	Struggling Student
Exams:	*Exams:*
Deals with anxiety by being prepared (having kept up with good notes and summaries throughout the semester and attempting practice exams at the end); reads the paper and its instructions about choices carefully; allocates time wisely so that each question is addressed; signposts answers with headings; and actually addresses the specific question posed in each part of the paper. Discusses underlying policy where the law is uncertain.	Responds to anxiety by last minute panic, cramming and desperate short-cuts; not attentive to detail in reading the exam paper; misjudges the timing of answers (either too much or too little per question); answers only part of the question; misses the point of the question; addresses matters not asked; is unable to articulate underlying policy as an aid to selection of authorities relevant to resolving the problem posed in the exam question.
Involvement in the Local Community:	*Involvement in the Local Community:*
Has part-time employment that allows demonstration of reliability, ability to work cooperatively with others and leadership potential, Undertakes part-time volunteer work in the community which broadens experiences and reveals a social conscience and sense of justice. Consistently gets good references.	Has a 'can't be bothered' attitude and an erratic work record. Rings in sick the day an assignment is due. Does not see employment or voluntary community service as a means of gaining new experiences and/or of demonstrating personal qualities of social responsibility, leadership and commitment. Unlikely to get good references.